Clarence Thomas

and the

Lost Constitution

Clarence Thomas

and the

Lost Constitution

Myron Magnet

New York • London

First American edition published in 2019 by Encounter Books,
an activity of Encounter for Culture and Education, Inc.,
a nonprofit, tax exempt corporation.
Encounter Books website address: www.encounterbooks.com

Manufactured in the United States and printed on
acid-free paper. The paper used in this publication meets
the minimum requirements of ANSI/NISO Z39.48–1992
(R 1997) (*Permanence of Paper*).

FIRST AMERICAN EDITION

LIBRARY OF CONGRESS CATALOGING-IN-PUBLICATION DATA
Names: Magnet, Myron, author.
Title: Clarence Thomas and the lost constitution / by Myron Magnet.
Description: New York : Encounter Books, 2019. |
Includes bibliographical references and index.
Identifiers: LCCN 2018050003 (print) | LCCN 2018051114 (ebook) |
ISBN 9781641770538 (ebook) | ISBN 9781641770521 (hardcover : alk. paper)
Subjects: LCSH: Thomas, Clarence, 1948- | United States. Supreme
Court--Officials and employees--Biography. |
African American judges--Biography. | Constitutional law--United States.
Classification: LCC KF8745.T48 (ebook) | LCC KF8745.T48 M34 2019 (print) |
DDC 347.73/2634 [B] --dc23
LC record available at https://lccn.loc.gov/2018050003

In Memoriam
Barbara Crehan Magnet
1946–2016

Contents

CHAPTER ONE

Our Crisis of Legitimacy

Well before his fellow Englishmen had grasped it, *Economist* founding editor Walter Bagehot observed that Britain really had two governments, one for show, one for real. The "dignified" government, he explained in his 1867 classic, *The English Constitution*, is the storied monarchy, with its pageantry of thrones and crowns, gilded coaches and showy guardsmen—but no power. The "efficient" government, which actually runs the realm, is the prime minister and his cabinet, mostly non-aristocrats who go about their business quietly in the shadows, bland men in sober suits (plus Jaguars with drivers today).

Something like that has developed in America, too. But while in Bagehot's England the two governments strengthened each other, the monarchy cloaking the efficient government in its venerable authority, in America the two have become so increasingly opposed that the disjunction now threatens a crisis of legitimacy. Though that crisis has long been brewing, the 1991 Senate hearings on Clarence Thomas's Supreme Court nomination first brought it into view, hazily. What was at stake to rouse such ferocity and lead the Judiciary Committee Democrats to sink to the politics of personal destruction, with almost no norm of decorum left intact, to smear Thomas's character rather than weigh his fitness as a jurist?

What led them to follow exactly the same playbook in the 2018 Brett Kavanaugh hearings, willing not only to ambush the judge at the eleventh hour with sordid, uncorroborated allegations of sexual transgressions as a teenager 36 years earlier but also to withhold from his chief accuser the key fact that she did not have to submit to humiliating public questioning in Washington but could have testified privately in her home state, as she requested? To those who used her as a mere tool of demolition, who farcically endorsed the hysterical shrieking of professional demonstrators in the gallery as "the sound of democracy," she was just as disposable as Kavanaugh, mere roadkill. Even the biased journalists dishing out fairy tales of yet more alleged debauchery and falsely inflating the main allegation into an attempted-rape charge, far graver than what the accuser described, included hardened veterans of the Thomas slander.

In the aftermath of this squalid spectacle, Left and Right are scarcely on speaking terms, and the anger isn't likely to fade anytime soon. That's because, as Americans are coming to recognize from the spotlight on the Court, Left and Right have visions of government so different that they can't be reconciled easily. One diagnostic index is Hillary Clinton's assertion that "You cannot be civil with a political party that wants to destroy what you stand for, what you care about." Another is Senator Cory Booker's claim that to support Kavanaugh is to be complicit with evil.[1] Yet a third is a recent poll showing that 68 percent of respondents think that only among like-minded people are they safe to say what they think about race or Islam, while 70 percent feel similarly constrained on sex and "gender," and 73 percent on immigration.[2] No wonder screaming mobs roam Washington and its suburbs, hounding Republican officials and their families out of restaurants and besieging a conservative broadcaster's house, while in New York, smirking, twentysomething activists mockingly harass a Fox News anchor in a subway car from which he can't escape, egging on fellow riders to taunt him threateningly for the villainy of his political incorrectness. *À la lanterne!*

———

How DID THIS divide happen? The answer lies in how immeasurably far we've traveled from our national ideal.

Start from the Founding Fathers' original vision of a democratic republic governed by the people's own elected representatives, charged with protecting citizens' inborn rights to life, property, and the liberty to work out their individual happiness themselves, in their families, communities, and states. Wary of government power after their colonial experience of arbitrary rule, the founders at first overcautiously formed a national regime so weak that it almost lost the Revolutionary War, and victory cost much more blood and suffering than in retrospect seemed necessary. So in 1787, they wrote a new Constitution, framing a central government strong enough to fight a war and fund it, but fenced round with limits to prevent its becoming the elective despotism they feared. As James Madison put it, because men are not angels—because they can (and do) rob, rape, kill, and conquer—they need a government to restrain and protect them, an "institution to make people do their duty." But since such an institution is made up of imperfect human beings with the same unruly passions as anyone else, "In framing a government of men over men, the great difficulty lies in this: You must first enable the government to control the governed; and in the next place, oblige it to control itself."[3]

We all learn about how the Constitution's framers accomplished that delicate balance through the three branches of government and the separation of their powers: democratically elected representatives frame laws to do the voters' will, which the elected president executes, unless the Supreme Court deems them unconstitutional. But that small government of limited and enumerated powers hasn't operated for nearly a century. All its parts still have their old names and appear to be carrying out their old functions. But in reality, a new kind of government has grown up inside the old structure, like those parasites hatched in another organism, which grow to maturity by eating up their host from within, until the adult creature bursts fully formed out of the host's carcass. The transformation that takes place is not an evolution but a usurpation.

As chapter 3 recounts, the governmental change occurred in three stages. First came the subversion of the Fourteenth Amendment, a largely forgotten but pivotal event in American racial and legal history, whose effects significantly shaped our subsequent national fate and still distort our jurisprudence. More well-known, thanks to a recent flood of scholarly and journalistic accounts, is the rise of a vast administrative state—government by executive-branch or independent agencies without a scintilla of constitutional legitimacy but nevertheless acting as a fourth branch of government, whose unelected, purportedly expert, bureaucrats make binding rules like a legislature, carry them out like an executive, and interpret and enforce them like a judiciary, all without a hint of separation of powers or checks and balances. Finally, the doctrine of the "living Constitution," first formulated by Woodrow Wilson and reaching its full development in the rights revolution unleashed by the Warren Court, swept away what spirit remained of the founders' governmental vision. As Wilson outlined the concept, the Court would sit as a permanent constitutional convention, continually making and remaking the law, to adapt, in a kind of Darwinian evolution, to changing circumstances. It would make up law, in Chief Justice Earl Warren's words, according to "the evolving standards of decency that mark the progress of a maturing society."[4]

This long process has divided Americans into camps with sharply different worldviews, as if from separate planets. The Right (to paint with a broad brush and thus oversimplify) still believes it lives in the old constitutional republic of limited and enumerated powers, as first outlined by James Madison, after deep study (summarized in *The Federalist*) of how and why ancient and modern republics succeeded or failed. It believes in democratic self-government, liberty, a laissez-faire responsibility for your individual fate, the justness of private property, a market economy, and American exceptionalism. It fears elective despotism through redistributive taxation, central economic planning, or overregulation. The legitimacy of this order, for the Right, rests on the evidence of history and on the consent of the people to the 1787 Constitution, the subsequent amendments, and the laws passed by their elected representatives.

Ever since the New Deal, those on the Right have sensed the American polity's transformation with growing discomfort, but around 2009, when the Tea Party movement mobilized, that discomfort turned to anger. It was a movement well named, signaling nostalgia for the old republican order; but beyond knowing that they opposed redistributive taxation and government by *diktat*, whether presidential or judicial, it took the Tea Partiers a while to realize how much of democratic self-government they had lost to the administrative state and an imperial Supreme Court. At first, the Right objected more to the policy outcomes than the process, but it now suspects that the process, according to its image of how the government is supposed to work, is illegitimate.

The Left, conversely, likes government by experts and elites. Greater enlightenment, which means not just more knowledge but consequently more compassion, assures that, in addition to perceiving what's best for the people, Leftist elites will naturally protect workers, "the disadvantaged," and a host of victim groups against over-powerful corporations and undeserved inequality, which to them is the essence of democracy. Experts will have the skill and the virtue to distribute wealth more fairly—that is, more equally—than the market, not according to self-interest but in the interest of social justice. Incalculable technological and moral progress has taken place since the founding, and those who are most up-to-date with it—especially well-educated administrators and justices from the Yale and Harvard Law Schools—are best suited to make just rules for a progressive society, to augment, correct, and sometimes nullify those broad directives made democratically by an electorate teeming with benighted deplorables, clinging to the guns and religion that the Second and First Amendments guarantee them. The unillusioned Left, by contrast, has traded in religion for politics, with the elect sheep divided from the infidel goats. Theirs is the legitimacy of the righteous.

For a half century, the Supreme Court, through increasingly fanciful legal reasoning, has handed the political Left victories in the culture wars—on race, sex, criminal justice, public order, schooling—that it would have found bruising, and sometimes impossible, to win through the constitutional legislative process. The Democratic Party does not want to have its fingers pried off this lever of incalculable power, especially now that Fox, Drudge, and the rest of the Internet have ended the elite's monopoly on print and broadcast news. In stark contrast, any conservative jurist, by definition, will believe that it is illegitimate for unelected justices with lifetime tenure to legislate from the bench in this Wilsonian manner. Irrespective of his or her own policy choices—even if, for instance, he believes that abortion or same-sex marriage should be legal—he is bound, if truly conservative, to think that the Constitution does not give the Supreme Court the authority to make such decisions. Matters of such gravity should be decided democratically, by the people acting through their elected representatives, whom they can fire if they disapprove. It's this irreconcilable disagreement that has turned Supreme Court judicial confirmations into shameful gladiatorial spectacles. And it's the reason that today's caricature-like embodiment of the Left is the haughty, elite Professor Obama, who always seems offended at the smell of the demos, while reality-TV construction boss Donald Trump personifies the Right, with his demotic, irreverent raspberry for any elite pretension.

———

JOINING THE COURT in 1991, Clarence Thomas brought with him the framers' vision of free, self-governing citizens forging their own fate. As chapter 2 dramatizes, from his own experience growing up in segregated Savannah, flirting with and rejecting black radicalism at college, and running one of the myriad administrative agencies that the Great Society had piled onto the New Deal's batch—an agency that supposedly advanced equality—he doubted that unelected experts and justices really did understand the moral arc of the universe better than the people themselves. He had seen how the rules and rulings they issued too often made lives worse, not better. So in the hundreds of opinions he has written in more than a quarter century on the Court—the most important of them explained in chapter 4 in non-lawyerly language that explains their constitutional reasoning and their historical background and importance—he has questioned the constitutional underpinnings of the new order and has tried to restore the limited, self-governing original one, as more legitimate, more just, and more free than the one that grew up in its stead. Like such other great dissenters as the first John Marshall Harlan or Antonin Scalia, he has blazed a trail to liberty that future justices can follow. And he is patient in waiting for the Court to catch up. "Think of Harlan in *Plessy*," he says of Harlan's lone dissent from the opinion of his brother justices that separate but equal facilities for black Americans are constitutional. "Do we quote from the majority or the dissent? It's the dissent that won the day—sixty years later!"[5]

A fierce Thomas critic, the late Judge Leon Higginbotham, once expressed disbelief that a fellow African American could be a conservative. "I am at a loss to understand," Higginbotham wrote, "what it is that so-called black conservatives are so anxious to conserve." He then got lost in confusion by defining conservatism only as Southern Democratic congressional resistance to the civil rights movement.[6] But, given that slavery and racism are ingrained in American history—with the Constitution itself counting a slave as three-fifths of a man, in the *realpolitik* compromise needed to get the Southern states to sign—it is an illuminating question nonetheless. It highlights the distinctiveness not only of black conservatism but of American conservatism more generally.

Modern conservatives often cite Edmund Burke as their intellectual godfather. But the gradual accretion of slow changes—political, legal, and cultural—that Burke saw as the moving force of history, with the useful or successful ones lasting for good reasons that we may have forgotten in the course of ages, but whose long acceptance gives them a legitimacy, a hold on the hearts of citizens, that we shouldn't lightly disturb, doesn't fit America's history. It is an apt description—or was, when Burke spoke—of England's millennium-long development, with its unwritten constitution made up of parliamentary statute and the case-by-case accumulation of the common law. But it applies less comfortably to a much younger nation with a written constitution and, as Thomas argues, no federal common law. To the extent America has had such a Burkean development, beyond its original settlers' inheritance of Western, especially British, civilization, it is the "living Constitution"—to American conservatives, an illegitimate distortion.

What American conservatives cherish is the founding idea. As Burke himself said of American culture, "a love of Freedom is the predominating feature which marks and distinguishes the whole.... This fierce spirit of Liberty is stronger in the English Colonies than in any other people on earth." After all, American Protestantism, born out of opposition to the official Church of England, "is a persuasion not only favorable to liberty, but built upon it." And with its "strong claim to natural liberty," it is "adverse to all implicit submission of mind and opinion."[7] As the following pages will show, that don't-tread-on-me independence and self-reliance, especially in intellectual matters, lies at the heart of Clarence Thomas's character, as he himself readily acknowledges.

But American liberty isn't negative. It's being left free for a purpose: for one's own pursuit of happiness, that completing idea of the American creed that Thomas Jefferson wrote into the Declaration of Independence. "Familiar words, easy to take for granted; easy to misconstrue," wrote the great English novelist V.S. Naipaul in the most lucid and moving explication of that phrase ever penned. "It is an elastic idea; it fits all men. It implies a certain kind of society, a certain kind of awakened spirit.... So much is contained in it: the idea of the individual, responsibility, choice, the life of the intellect, the idea of vocation and perfectibility and achievement. It is an immense human idea. It cannot be reduced to a fixed system. It cannot generate fanaticism. But it is known to exist; and because of that, other more rigid systems in the end blow away."[8]

These are the ideals that American conservatives wish to conserve. They are ideals—as the founders well knew but could not bring to fruition in their lifetimes—that apply to all men, regardless of their color. They are the ideals that Clarence Thomas cherishes and tries to make more perfect in his career on the Supreme Court.

———

I AM not a constitutional law professor but a writer, whose last book, *The Founders at Home: The Building of America, 1735–1817,* told the story of the American founding through a series of crisp biographies. I wanted to find out, from reading the Founding Fathers' letters, journals, and speeches, as well as studying their deeds, just what kind of republic they thought they were creating. But solving that puzzle raised further questions. We no longer have the republic of their imagination. How and why did we lose it? Because something meaner superseded it, how can we at least in part restore their magnificent self-governing nation of liberty?

The following pages try to answer those questions. Part of the solution, I argue in chapter 5, is that a free, self-governing republic requires a culture of liberty, capable of producing responsible, self-reliant citizens, adverse to all implicit submission of mind and opinion, in Burke's resonant phrase.

So I thought of Clarence Thomas, with whom I have been acquainted for more than two decades but did not interview for this book, by no means an authorized account. Despite the justice's reputation for silence—he famously almost never asks questions during the Court's oral argument—he has produced volumes of Court opinions, speeches, articles, symposia, and an insightful, self-examining memoir, *My Grandfather's Son*—all of which compose a faithful and detailed picture of his worldview. He is precisely the kind of character I had in mind, though one can become independent and self-reliant without quite as much adversity as he has surmounted, and he has spent his professional life thinking about just the questions I was asking, from a position that allows him to nudge the nation in the right direction, when so much in the culture is pushing in the wrong way. President George H.W. Bush knew whereof he spoke when he pronounced, at Thomas's swearing-in as a justice, "America is blessed to have a man of this character serve on its highest court."[9] So this is a life-and-works book in which the life and works mutually illuminate each other to a greater than usual degree and add up to a whole, I hope you will conclude, that is greater than the sum of its parts.

CHAPTER TWO

The Making
of a Justice

At the end of each Supreme Court term, around Independence Day, Justice Thomas likes to take his clerks to tour the Civil War battlefield at Gettysburg. By then, long hours of intense, closely researched debate, along with the almost parental care that the justice and his wife, Virginia, have lavished upon them, have melded the young lawyers into something like family. They have spent part of the year on Fourteenth Amendment questions, but now it's time for a closer look at the realities the amendment addresses. "I thought it would be important for my clerks not just to talk about the Fourteenth Amendment, not just to talk about the equal protection clause," explained Thomas in a 2016 Heritage Foundation lecture, marking his twenty-fifth anniversary on the Court, "but to go and feel it—to see the place, to see what this was about. Why did people die? To go where Lincoln delivered the Gettysburg Address, where he implores us, the living, to make it worthwhile, this experiment to which these people had given the last full measure." Because, he concludes, what the war, the address, and the amendment were all about was a magnificent ideal: "the perfectibility of this great republic."[1]

That same ideal of republican perfectibility—the full realization of Jefferson's proposition that all men are created equal—lies at the heart of Thomas's career on the nation's highest court, too. Lincoln had urged his Gettysburg audience to rededicate themselves to that ideal to spark a new birth of freedom, which perhaps would have occurred, had not some crazed, failed actor felt called to blow out the noblest brain of his age five days after the South's surrender. History is filled with what-ifs: but had Lincoln lived, perhaps his visionary genius, prophetic oratory, and iron determination would have made Reconstruction succeed, investing black Southerners permanently with all the civil rights of American citizenship, as the heroic president intended. That's why biographer Richard Brookhiser calls Lincoln the "Founders' Son": the Great Emancipator understood the Founding Fathers' vision of liberty and equality before the law with a seer's acuity and aimed to bring it to pass more completely than existing circumstances had allowed the founders themselves to do.[2]

But Southern segregationists, with the connivance of Lincoln's successor, Andrew Johnson, violently derailed his plan soon after his assassination and prolonged racial oppression for nearly another century, distorting race relations in the whole nation to this day. It's in this sense, as Thomas works to fulfill Lincoln's task of extending the unalienable rights of the Declaration of Independence to all Americans, that it's not fanciful to think of the justice as the founders' grandson.

———

How THOMAS could become so historically consequential is a story that really begins with his actual grandfather, Myers Anderson. Thomas was born on June 23, 1948, in Pinpoint, Georgia, a tiny creekside hamlet founded by freed slaves 11 miles southeast of Savannah, where the men caught crabs and raked oysters and the women picked and shucked them in a little cinder-block factory. Despite its poverty, Thomas's early childhood in the woods and swamps seemed idyllic to him, something like an African American Huck Finn. But

when he was six, his younger brother and cousin, playing with match-
es, burned down their kerosene-lit shanty, and his mother, who had
divorced his father when Thomas was two, took her two sons to live
in the "foulest kind of urban squalor" of inner-city Savannah, leaving
their elder sister behind with relatives. In their cramped apartment,
with its cracked and stinking outdoor toilet, single faucet, and lino-
leum kitchen floor laid directly on the earth, Thomas knew "hunger
without the prospect of eating and cold without the prospect of
warmth," he recounts in his vivid memoir, *My Grandfather's Son*.[3]
But after one awful winter, his mother, exhausted and demoralized
from her $10-a-week housecleaning job, sent the two little boys, their
meager wardrobes packed in one paper bag apiece, to live with her
father and stepmother, two and a half blocks away.

That short walk, all by themselves, took the children to a different
world. Myers and Christine Anderson lived in a sparkling-white,
sparkling-clean two-bedroom cinder-block house that they had built
themselves for $600. It boasted hardwood floors, a fridge flowing with
milk and soda, a stove, washer, and, a special luxury to Thomas, por-
celain indoor plumbing. Though barely literate, Anderson had started
his own wood-, ice-, and coal-delivery business, which, by the time
his grandsons came to live with him, had evolved into a heating-oil
company, with himself making the deliveries and his wife taking the
orders and keeping the books. Thomas was surprised to learn that
the business had never grossed more than $7,000 a year—especially
considering how hard his driven grandfather worked, starting before
dawn every day. But it was enough to keep the little family of four in
comfort and security.

The Andersons had had no children together, though as teenagers
before marriage each had had out-of-wedlock offspring, including
Thomas's mother. Anderson himself had been born to a single mother,
and "he resented his father's lack of interest in him," Thomas remarks,
no less than his grandsons resented their absent father. The boys used
to ask themselves "how a man could show no interest in his own children," Thomas recalls. "I still wonder." They would conclude by "saying

that the only father we ever had was our grandfather," Thomas says. "What I am is what he made me."[4]

———

CERTAINLY, ANDERSON, then in his 40s, took to child-rearing with born-again zeal, though whether to plug the hole in his heart left by his own father's absence, or to atone for his own early sins of omission as an unwed father, or to fill up the void in his otherwise model but childless household, as Thomas believes, is unknowable. Having made himself into a paragon of self-discipline and hard work, he was determined to mold the boys in his image, through a rigid structure of rules, good manners, high expectations, and moral maxims so vivid and oft-repeated that before long the boys were lip-syncing as their grandfather pronounced them. "Old Man Can't is dead—I helped bury him," he would say, or "Any job worth doing is worth doing right," or "Waste not, want not," or "Play the hand you're dealt"—a laudable call to face reality and cope with it head-on, without self-pity, very different from the mind-set of such celebrated younger black memoirists as Barack Obama or Ta-Nehisi Coates. It was a tough school of virtue, aimed at giving the boys the tools to surpass their grandfather's achievements and get "coat-and-tie jobs."[5]

As part of his own self-reinvention, Anderson had embraced Catholicism, rejecting the traditional black Baptist church's ecstatic emotionalism in favor of order, dogma, and ritual. He sent his grandsons to Catholic school and pushed them to serve as altar boys, slapping Thomas across the room one Sunday for starting for church with unshined shoes. Anderson liked the structured environment of St. Benedict the Moor school, with its neat uniforms, its no-nonsense demand for achievement, and its housekeeping chores for each pupil. The mostly Irish Franciscan nuns taught their students that since God made all men equal, segregation was wrong. "There was always this underlying sense that we were entitled to be a full participant in 'We the People,'" Thomas recalls. "That was the way the nuns, who were all immigrants, explained it to us. There was never any doubt that we were inherently equal—it said so in the Declaration of Independence." Perhaps for that teaching, segregated Savannah's whites called the nuns "the nigger sisters."[6]

Once Thomas reached fourth grade, Anderson put him to work after school and on Saturdays, taking orders and helping deliver oil. Shortly afterward, grandfather and grandsons began building a cinder-block house on 60 fallow south-Georgia acres that Thomas's great-great-great-grandfather had bought in the 1870s, right across from the plantation where his family had been enslaved for over 100 years and from which he had then been emancipated. Thereafter, the family spent the whole of every summer vacation on "the farm," where the boys worked from dawn till dark, clearing fields in the brutal Georgia heat, mending fences, helping to plow and harvest and, from time to time, to butcher a hog. "As my grandfather said, we all were going to be raised in the ways of slavery times," Thomas recalls.[7] The point was not just the food that the family ate the rest of the year: Anderson knew how toxic inner-city street culture could be, and he wanted to keep the boys from its influence by filling up every hour with parochial school, homework, oil delivery, and farm work.

Thomas and his siblings constitute a natural experiment in the effects of such a caring, supervised, value-laden upbringing, compared with a more typical poor, fatherless childhood. It is the difference between freedom and victimhood. He and his brother both became upwardly mobile successes, though a heart attack killed his brother while jogging at age 50. His high-school-dropout sister, left behind as drugs and crime invaded Pinpoint, went on welfare, as Thomas told eminent journalist Juan Williams in 1980. "She gets mad when the mailman is late with her welfare check," Thomas said, explaining his opposition to the dole. "That is how dependent she is. What's worse is that now her kids feel entitled to the check too. They have no motivation for doing better or getting out of that situation."[8]

He was more right than he knew, for though his sister later got off welfare and got a GED and a menial job, her son took to selling cocaine. "Mark, please, you got them pretty little kids. Please," Thomas would beg his nephew, from the depths of his own early experience of fatherlessness.[9] But to no avail, for the oft-jailed Mark finally drew a 30-year prison sentence in 1999. Thomas took in Mark's six-year-old son, became his surrogate father, and sent him to private school, as his grandfather had done for him.

———

SEGREGATION-CONSTRICTED Savannah was almost as small as Pinpoint. "Segregation created fear," Thomas told his Heritage Foundation audience, and that fear kept black children from venturing beyond the ghetto.[10] Little wonder, since the Ku Klux Klan held a Savannah march, in white robes and witches' hats, as late as 1960, when Thomas was 12. And segregation played a powerful role in his gradually maturing worldview. "When you live in a system where the government tells you that you can't walk across a park, you can't drink out of a particular water fountain, you can't vote, . . . you can't go to a certain library, you can't go to a certain school, you begin to think about the use and misuse of governmental power," Thomas said in a 2018 speech.[11] It took a while to ripen, but it was a firsthand, negative lesson in the blessings of liberty.

Still, in his childhood's little world, his sharpest memory of racism, which would loom ever larger to him as he grew up, is the taunt from fellow black kids that he was "ABC—America's Blackest Child."[12] All that changed when, after a spell at the local Catholic high school, he persuaded his grandfather to send him to Saint John Vianney, a boarding school for prospective Catholic priests, which he entered at 16 in autumn 1964, one of two black students in an otherwise all-white institution on Isle of Hope, just outside Savannah. There he first encountered the anxiety of inferiority that, as an adult, he warned would beset the supposed beneficiaries of affirmative action. "We had always believed we could do as well as whites if we were only given a fair shake," he writes—"but what if it turned out that we weren't good enough after all?" Thomas worked as hard as his grandfather had taught him to and earned such stellar grades that his yearbook photo bore the caption "blew the test, only a 98."[13]

Even so, his smirking schoolmates needled him with racist taunts. "After lights out someone would yell, 'Smile, Clarence, so we can see you.' The statement wasn't the bad part, it was no one saying 'Shut up.'"[14] When, after Herculean effort, he won a Latin prize—a statuette of Saint Jude—someone broke off its head, and broke it again after he glued it back on. He glued it a third time, and his tormentors gave up. The saint now protects his Supreme Court desk. So touchy did he understandably become that when the school's rector advised him to learn to speak standard English—his speech smacked of the Gullah dialect of the Georgia barrier islands, similar to West Indian creole, that he had first learned—he took it as a racist slap. Much later, he learned that the rector had given the same advice to white students with thick Southern drawls.[15]

But only when he enrolled in the Immaculate Conception Seminary in Kansas City, Missouri, did racism derail him. With one of his few black fellow students, he agonized over the church's failure to condemn racism and segregation, a failure that he felt subverted its moral claims. A classmate's brutal response to the news of Martin Luther King's shooting during Thomas's first year—"I hope the son of a bitch dies"—"finished off my vocation," Thomas recalls. "This was a man of God, mortally stricken by an assassin's bullet, and one preparing for the priesthood had wished evil upon him."[16] When he came home and announced his resolve to leave the seminary, his disappointed grandfather, who had worked so hard and proudly to pay for his schooling and whom Thomas had long before promised not to quit the path to becoming Savannah's first black priest, turned him out of the house. To Thomas's lasting regret, grandfather and grandson never really made up, and Anderson, who died in 1983 (a month before Thomas's equally beloved step-grandmother), didn't live to see Thomas join the high court. Abandoned by his father, then by his mother, and then thrown out by the grandfather who had rescued him: some wounds can't heal.

———

A SUMMER JOB at a Savannah paper company, where he choked down his inner rage at his white coworkers' pervasive racism, turned him, he says, into "an angry black man." As a transfer student at mostly white Holy Cross in 1968—with a scholarship and work-study job at the elite Massachusetts school, as his grandfather no longer paid the bills—he grew angrier still, adopting the rhetoric, gestures, and army-surplus garb of the sixties' black student radical. Awaiting the revolution that would purify a U.S. culture "irretrievably tainted by racism," he then believed, he and his small band of fellow black undergrads put on the "swagger [and] sense of moral superiority" of "the aggrieved and the righteous."[17]

"It would not be until I was exposed to the most fortunate and best educated in our society that I would be informed that all this time I had been a victim," he recalled in a 1995 speech. "You can imagine what it was like when I returned home to Savannah, and informed my grandparents that with the education I had received because of their tremendous foresight and sacrifice, I had discovered our oppressed and victimized status in society. Needless to say relations were quite strained, and our vacation visits were somewhat difficult. My grandfather was no victim and he didn't send me to school to become one."[18]

———

EVEN SO, his critical judgment never wholly deserted him. He began to see—but not to say—that the conventional left-wing nostrums for uplifting black Americans might backfire. Holy Cross was doing no favor to many of the black students it admitted in increasing numbers under affirmative action, he thought. Smart but unprepared, they too often got bad grades or flunked out. "Why, I asked, were these gifted young people being sacrificed on the altar of an abstract theory of social justice," when they would have flourished closer to home or in all-black colleges? Those affirmative-action beneficiaries who succeeded tended to be the light-skinned children of middle-class families who needed no extra boost and who, with their own brand of racism, looked down on darker, poorer blacks like himself.[19]

Despite his ambivalence, he went to an April 1970 march on Harvard Square to protest the Vietnam War and show support for "America's domestic political prisoners," such as Black Panther murderers. The march turned into a riot—complete with looting, arson, and nearly 200 injured kids and cops—to Thomas's horror. Back at Holy Cross the next morning, he had what he calls a "road to Damascus" moment. He begged God to purge his heart of the "rage and resentment that threatened to wreck my academic career and my life," shrinking him to a knee-jerk stereotype mouthing empty slogans and accomplishing nothing. To change the world, he realized, he'd have to change himself first; he'd have to man up and play as best he could the hand he was dealt—a hand containing, he acknowledged, much better cards than his grandfather had ever held. Yes, he had gone through a radical phase at college, he acknowledged, and he knew radicalism's cant from inside. But "then I grew up."[20]

———

BY THE TIME he reached Yale Law School in 1971, his politically incorrect views on race were hardening fast—and it's worth emphasizing that, as with so many ex-radicals, he had had to *think* his way to conservativism, not realizing that the maxims and example of his grandfather, a proud Democrat and NAACP member, *were* conservatism. With him, as with many former radicals, that thinking involved a meditation on the real-world results of the radical nostrums he had once espoused. He looked squarely and honestly at the practical outcomes of his virtuous intentions. "I marched. I protested. I asked the government to help black people," Thomas ruefully remarked in 1980. "I did all those things. But it hasn't worked. It isn't working. And someone needs to say that."[21] Given the counterexample of his grandfather's virtues, he was a natural spokesman for them, especially as the cultural changes of the 1960s were fast undermining them.

He and his college sweetheart had married just after his college graduation (they divorced in 1984), and the birth of their son just when the NAACP's Boston school busing lawsuit headlined the news in 1973 made him inwardly vow that, if public school systems planned to bus poor black kids for an hour each day to a white school just as bad as the black one right around the corner, he would send baby Jamal to private school, whatever the cost, rather than offer him as one more sacrifice to a feel-good but harebrained social experiment. And so he did. Investigating why so many black law graduates flunked the bar exam, he discovered that, with each question graded by a separate scorer and the test takers identified by numbers alone, discrimination was an unlikely answer, despite the claims of yet another NAACP lawsuit. The test's "adverse impact" on black test takers showed only the culpability of those who had set these unready kids up for failure, he thought. His most painful discovery, though, was that Yale Law's affirmative-action push starting in 1969 made employers view the school's subsequent black grads as inferior, harming even those who, like Thomas, had earned good grades. That Yale had admitted him in part because he was black, he writes, "was the soft underbelly of my career."[22]

"I couldn't get a job," Thomas told a University of Kansas Law School audience in 1996—or at least not a law-firm job that would make him a lawyer, rather than a kind of pro bono social worker, advertising the firm's righteous intentions.[23] What was "a Yale law degree worth when it bore the taint of racial preference?" he asks in his memoir. In answer, he peeled a 15-cent price tag off a cigar package and stuck it onto his framed diploma, before stashing it in the cellar forever.[24]

At last, Missouri's Republican attorney general John Danforth saw his worth and offered him a job, which Thomas accepted on condition that he'd be treated no differently from the other assistant AGs. Danforth, true to his equal-opportunity promise, "ignored the hell out of me," Thomas gratefully recalls.[25] In his stint in the criminal appeals division, the young lawyer lost his last radical illusion about race. Jailed blacks were not political prisoners, suffering oppression by "the man," he found. A black man who made a black woman submit to rape and sodomy by holding a blade to her little boy's throat was just a thug. "This case, I later learned, was far from unusual: it turned out that blacks were responsible for almost 80 percent of violent crimes committed against blacks, and killed over 90 percent of black murder victims," he writes. "This was a bitter pill to swallow." But swallow it he did, growing permanently skeptical of radicalism's fictitious assertions and conspiracy theories.[26]

Finally, he read a review of Thomas Sowell's *Race and Economics*, which reassured him that he and his grandfather weren't the only African Americans to believe that black advancement required self-reliance, education, work skills, and pride in achievement—all subverted, Sowell argued, by job quotas, charity subsidies, and preferential treatment. That recognition meant giving up the illusion "that whites, having caused our problems, should be responsible for solving them instantly," Thomas realized. On the contrary, "blacks could never hope to improve their lives until they took responsibility for them."[27]

———

AFTER DANFORTH'S 1976 election to the U.S. Senate, Thomas, richer in experience but still poor in purse, went to work for chemical giant Monsanto's law department, which only partly repaired his finances and galled him with the sense that he was just a token affirmative-action hire. Though his bosses soon perceived his talent and offered a promotion and a raise, he nevertheless jumped at the chance of going to Washington to join Danforth's Senate staff. His life ambition, he realized, was not to make money. "The reason I became a lawyer was to make sure that individuals who did not have access to this society, gained access," he explained. "I may differ with others on how best to do that, but the objective has always been to include those who have been excluded."[28] He worried, however, that if he clearly stressed the crucial centrality of black self-reliance to achieve that end, an opinion he'd hitherto cloaked under "the similar-sounding views of Malcolm X and the Black Muslims," he'd earn the same condemnation that black

activists poured on Sowell. So he temporized, accepting Danforth's offer with the proviso that he wouldn't work on race or civil rights issues.
But ultimately, he knew, he'd have to follow his grandfather's maxim
that "you have to stand up for what you believe in."[29]

His mask fell by accident at the end of 1980, after he'd read through
Sowell's works, registered as a Republican, and voted for Ronald Reagan, whose promise to end the racial social engineering of the last two
decades coincided with Thomas's belief that "blacks would be better off
if they were left alone instead of being used as guinea pigs for the foolish
schemes of dream-killing politicians and their ideological acolytes."[30]
Government, he had come to think—like Reagan—was part of the
problem, not the solution. At a San Francisco conference on race, where
organizer Sowell had asked him to join a panel on education policy, he
told fellow attendee Juan Williams his views on welfare, illustrated by
his sister's current situation—unguardedly, without any thought that
he might be giving an interview to a heavyweight journalist. Back in
Danforth's office, he was flabbergasted when a *Washington Post* pho-
tographer called to take his picture for Williams's column recounting
his comments, to appear the next day.

The abuse followed as expected. But what also followed was an
offer in 1981 to head the civil rights division of the Reagan Education
Department, clearly (and offensively to him) because of his race, since
he was no education professional. He asked a friend for advice, expecting—and hoping for—dissuasion. "Aren't you tired of just *talking* about
problems, Clarence?" his friend challenged, to his surprise. "Wouldn't
you like to try doing something about them, for a change? Put up or
shut up." He put up—a decision that led inexorably to the high court.[31]

———

His nine years as a federal official—at the Department of Education
till 1982 and then as chairman of the Equal Employment Opportunity
Commission until 1990—not only gave him ample data to support his
unorthodox views but also a concrete way to stop government from

making America's race problems worse. Poring over the Department of Education's numbers, he saw that almost half of black kids in white colleges failed to graduate on time, if at all, and very few graduates ranked in the top half of the class. Few took the math, science, and engineering courses that increasingly led to success in a high-tech economy. Maybe they'd do better in historically black colleges, Thomas opined to a senior bureaucrat. Those segregated institutions had no right to exist, the official huffily snapped, toeing the line of the mainstream civil rights groups. Thomas wasn't convinced.

The data on black performance in integrated high schools told an equally dispiriting tale of dropout, failure, poor course choices, and misbehavior, though the better achievement of the girls partly masked the dismal washout of the boys. His staffers could provide no data showing that integrated primary and secondary schools helped black students learn more than all-black schools. The department had no interest in that question, staffers told him, since the point of integration and forced busing wasn't education but ultimately the integration of America's neighborhoods. By contrast, "I didn't care which schools blacks attended, so long as they received a good education," Thomas wrote. "You don't need to sit next to a white person to learn how to read and write."[32]

Once he had cleaned up the administrative mess he had inherited at EEOC and had named himself executive director as well as chairman, to take full responsibility for results, Thomas set about changing the commission's approach to employment-discrimination claims. Out went class action lawsuits based on alleged patterns and practices of discrimination, demonstrated by statistics that showed only outcomes, not necessarily any intent to discriminate by race, as opposed to perfectly justified discrimination by qualification or accomplishment. Only individual cases of proven racial discrimination interested him. "The most vulnerable unit in our society is the individual. And blacks, in my opinion being one of the most vulnerable groups, should fight like hell to preserve individual freedoms so people can't gang up on us," he told Juan Williams, like him a highly successful, deeply thoughtful black professional and by then the journalist he trusted most. "Suppose we did band together, group against group—which group do you think would win?"[33]

Speaking more broadly, anyone who thinks the EEOC or any other federal body can make amends for past discrimination by putting a thumb on the scale in favor of blacks is deluded. "There is no governmental solution," he told Williams during his time at EEOC. As illustration, he told Williams a boyhood story of playing blackjack, when one player rightly accused the boy who kept winning of supplying marked cards. All the players grabbed for the pennies in the pot, seizing whatever they could get, compounding the original unfairness, so that no one could ever determine who was owed what. Loud shouts and threats ensued; but as the boys wanted to keep playing rather than fight, they brought out a new deck and restarted the game, simply accepting the unfair distribution of the stakes. So if America had stacked the deck against blacks until the 1964 Civil Rights Act, how could it begin to determine how to redistribute the stakes justly? The only workable course is to resume the game under the new, fair rules.[34]

"I would be lying to you if I said that I didn't want sometimes to be able to cheat in favor of those of us who were cheated," Thomas told Williams, especially since all the Civil Rights Act did was to "stop stopping us." But as history shows, all American minority groups have to forge their success for themselves, person by person. For now, Thomas ruefully continued, "There is nothing you can do to get past black skin. I don't care how educated you are, how good you are at what you do—you'll never have the same contacts or opportunities, you'll never be seen as equal to whites." But despite this disadvantage, in now-equal-opportunity America, blacks can make their way upward, like all previously despised hyphenated Americans. "The issue is economics—not who likes you."[35]

In any event, a thumb on the scale in favor of one group disadvantages another. "Playing that game builds up racial conflict," Thomas observed—an insight that might have profited former attorney general Eric Holder and his boss, President Obama, as would Thomas's caution that group favoritism violates the Constitution, "which says you are to protect an individual's rights no matter what. Once you say that we can violate somebody else's rights in order to make up for what happened to blacks or other races or other groups in history, then you are setting a precedent for having certain circumstances in which you can overlook another person's rights."[36]

———

THAT REVERENCE for the Constitution—sown in grammar school, where the nuns made their pupils recite the document's preamble by heart—took deep root in Thomas during his EEOC tenure, when he hired as special assistants Ken Masugi and John Marini, students of political philosopher Harry Jaffa, the West Coast oracle of Leo Strauss's natural-law political theory. Masugi recalls that Thomas told him, "I have to spend my days working for the agency, and I don't have time to think." So he asked the two academics to help him fill that gap in his education. The result, says Masugi, was that he and Marini became high-level tutors, guiding Thomas's reading and expounding the recommended Strausian texts, giving him, without knowing what lay in store, the education of a justice.[37]

They conveyed the heart of Jaffa's version of Straus: that the Declaration of Independence, with its proposition that man's inborn natural rights preexist any government formed to guarantee those rights, lies at the heart of the American project; that the framers saw the Constitution as the governmental machinery to "secure the blessings of liberty to ourselves and our posterity," as its preamble says and as the Declaration promised; that it was Lincoln who understood, as he said in eulogizing Henry Clay, that the founders, "cast into life where slavery was already widely spread and deeply seated, . . . did not perceive, as I think no wise man has perceived, how it could be at *once* eradicated, without producing a greater evil, even to the cause of liberty itself"; and how, whatever Jefferson's proposition that all men are created equal might mean, it certainly means, as Lincoln put it in 1858, that, while "the negro is not our equal in color—perhaps not in many other respects; still, in the right to put into his mouth the bread that his own hands have earned, he is the equal of every other man, white or black."[38]

So Thomas was intellectually prepared when President George H.W. Bush, who'd marked him as a potential jurist when he was still at the Education Department, nominated him for a seat on the D.C. Circuit Court of Appeals in 1989, and emotionally ready for the stiff left-wing opposition to his anti-affirmative-action views. But an extravagant document demand from crafty Senate Judiciary Committee chief Joe Biden gave him pause—he thought it as much a fishing expedition as the committee staff's subsequent three-hour taped interview with him—and Biden's later warning that he'd support *this* nomination but would balk at ever confirming him to the Supreme Court flabbergasted him. The shrewd Democrat could read the political tea leaves better than he could—as he saw when President Bush nominated him to the high court in July 1991, just 15 months after he joined the appeals court. In retrospect, said former White House counsel C. Boyden Gray in 2016 (two years before the ex-president died), Bush "views this as one of the best things he ever did."[39]

———

THE PARTISAN NASTINESS of his confirmation is legendary. With Biden as ringleader, Democrats had tasted blood when they killed Robert Bork's nomination to the Court 21 months earlier, in order to keep control of what had become a potent, if wildly unconstitutional, law*making* body rather than a law-judging body, as the following pages will show in detail. Now they aimed for Thomas's scalp too, determined to maintain the Court as their own partisan, magical rights-creating machine, especially the rights to abortion and affirmative action, in those days as much for women as for blacks.

Thomas's White House and Senate supporters warned him what was in store at the very beginning of what turned out to be a three-month ordeal. The left-wing activists "are going to throw the kitchen sink at you," predicted one presidential aide—and indeed the Alliance for Justice, an oddly tax-exempt far-left lobbying group, had already been doing opposition research on him for two years.[40] Sure enough, the day after his nomination, a liberal national church council denounced him as anti–civil rights, and the National Abortion Rights League anathematized him for not chanting its creed. Thomas kept wondering, "What would they cook up against me?" As the abuse intensified, he increasingly felt trapped in some Kafkaesque world where people were ransacking his garbage and "poring through files and documents with no other purpose than to destroy you as a person."[41]

"I felt under siege the entire summer," Thomas told his old boss and biggest supporter, Senator Danforth. "These people are going to try to kill me. I hadn't done anything to them, but they are going to try to kill me." And that's now par for the course in the confirmation process in a government that no longer understands its constitutional functions and limits.[42] The Senate needs someone of the stature and authority of George Washington to tell them, as the great president starchily made clear to the senators at the very start of his administration, that "advise and consent" really means "consent."[43] The Constitutional Convention over which he presided certainly didn't mean it as a veto on ideological—or, as he would put it, "factional"—grounds.

Thomas gamely swatted away false rumors, such as anti-Semitism, and in a pre-confirmation interview, he dealt easily with one senator's challenge to his natural-law views by explaining that the founders had written the philosophy that "all law is based on some sense of moral principles inherent in the nature of human beings" into the Declaration of Independence. Those inborn principles, he noted, explain why the senator wouldn't "consider having a human-being sandwich for lunch instead of, say, a turkey sandwich." The senator changed the subject.[44]

———

THE SENATE JUDICIARY COMMITTEE probed him for five days in September, with Democrats—"armed with long lists of trick questions prepared by law professors and activists," he recalls—especially focused on the 1973 *Roe v. Wade* decision that legalized abortion nationwide. After a 7–7 committee vote on September 27, 1991, the full Senate prepared to vote on his confirmation.

But then, up sprang law professor Anita Hill, whom Thomas, at a friend's request, had hired at the Education Department when she was one year out of Yale Law. She charged in a written statement given to the committee by the Alliance for Justice that Thomas had sexually harassed her with sordid sexual remarks and with repeated tries to date her despite rebuffs. In the statement—which a Senate staffer had told her might well prompt Thomas to withdraw from consideration without Hill's name ever being publicly disclosed but which was leaked from the committee and trumpeted by *Newsday*, *USA Today*, National Public Radio, and a host of other outlets on October 6, and amplified by Hill in a televised news conference the next day—the young accuser presented herself as devout, modest, and conservative, though Thomas recalled that she was not religious and was an argumentative, pro-racial-quota ideologue who avowed that she detested President Reagan, so much so that he could only hire her as a career, rather than a political, appointee.[45]

On Tuesday, October 8, as the television stations chattered about Hill nonstop, Thomas's Senate supporters requested a postponement of the scheduled vote so that the nominee could answer her charges. "She had gone on for three days in a row without one volley of criticism," recalled Judiciary Committee member Alan Simpson. "She was the toast of America, the beleaguered one who had come forward, the martyred one, the aggrieved, and he was just the ogre of the piece."[46] Now, Thomas's allies urged, it was time for him to fight.

He was angry enough to do so.

With *Native Son* and *To Kill a Mockingbird* echoing in his mind, he chafed at having the hackneyed racist stereotype mobilized against him: "*You can't trust a black man around women.*" In his Deep South childhood, he'd feared the KKK, ready to lynch any black man for sexual misconduct, so "I'd grown up hyperconscious of the need to avoid even the appearance of such impropriety," he says. But now he "was being pursued not by bigots in white robes but by left-wing zealots draped in flowing sanctimony," wielding Hill as their tool. He went back into the Senate Caucus Room on Friday, October 11, and vehemently denied Hill's charges, pointing out that at the EEOC—a body explicitly devoted to equal employment opportunity for women, among others—he "adamantly condemned sex harassment" and took "swift and decisive action" against any employee who committed it, summarily firing one subordinate who called a colleague "a faggot."[47] Perhaps more important, he indicted the gladiatorial circus that the confirmation process had become, upbraiding the Democratic senators for subjecting him to a 103-day, un-American ordeal of lies and slime, and refusing to answer further questions about "the intimate parts of my private life," which "will remain just that, private." He left the senators speechless.

———

THEN IT WAS Hill's turn. Thomas didn't stay to watch her performance but went home and listened to music. I saw her on television, and, watching her prim, modest, Sunday-school-teacher demeanor, I couldn't help thinking of Joseph L. Mankiewicz's classic film, *All About Eve*. In it, the scheming young title character presents herself as an innocent, injured, idealistic ingénue as she manipulates her way to success at the expense of her patrons. Only the maid sees the truth: "Oh bruthuh," says actress Thelma Ritter in the purest Old Brooklynese. "What a story! Everything but the bloodhounds snappin' at her rear end."

Hill's was a story replete with details inconceivable for so prim a lady to have invented. Thomas, she charged, had described to her in technicolor detail a pornographic film featuring one Long Dong Silver, named for the endowment that raised him to stardom in his genre. "He spoke about acts that he had seen in pornographic films involving such matters as women having sex with animals and films showing group sex or rape scenes," she said in her sworn statement to the Senate Judiciary Committee.[48] In another vividly specific charge, Hill claimed that

Thomas had asked her who had put a pubic hair on his Coke can. Who could make up such bizarrely detailed allegations?

No sooner had Hill finished than Senator Danforth phoned Thomas and implored him to return to the committee that very evening, to block Hill's lurid story from dominating the next day's news. He wearily agreed. When the committee reconvened at 8 PM, he went in and told the senators, with the weight of all his experience of segregationist Savannah, that their hearing was "a circus,…a national disgrace,…a high-tech lynching for uppity blacks who in any way deign to think for themselves, to do for themselves, to have different ideas." When he was done, he recalls, his words "seemed to hang in the air…like the smoke from a bomb that had just exploded." Democratic senators as…*racist*?

Like a nightmare that doesn't end, the hearings resumed the next morning. Senator Orrin Hatch, questioning Thomas, proceeded to create his own explosion, quieter than Thomas's of the night before but perhaps more devastating. "People hearing yesterday's testimony are probably wondering how could this quiet, you know, retiring woman know about something like Long Dong Silver," Hatch remarked, with considerable embarrassment. "Did you tell her that?" No he didn't, Thomas replied, and he had no idea how she heard it. But Hatch did, and he explained. A 1988 sexual harassment case—whose transcript lay in the EEOC files, which Hill had asked to consult after she had left the commission—had discussed that very performer, even including a photograph of the feature in question. So bookworm Hill wouldn't have had to leave a law library to learn such lurid details. Hatch also noted that the pubic hair on the Coke can echoed a line in the bestselling novel and blockbuster movie *The Exorcist*.[49]

———

THAT ANSWERED a question troubling many Americans—who also wondered, if Thomas had so harassed Hill, why had she followed him from the Education Department to EEOC? Similarly, federal judge Laurence Silberman, a friend of Thomas's, had wondered outside the committee room why someone who had been sexually harassed would invite the harasser up to her apartment for a drink after he drove her home.[50] But what about the graver question of why might Hill lie under oath?

Senator Alan Simpson got a possible answer to that question later that day when cross-examining Hill's corroborating witness, Susan Hoerchner, who equivocated about whether she herself had ever filed a sexual harassment complaint, until confronted with evidence that she had forced a fellow administrative-law judge to resign by such an accusation, demonstrating the lethal power of such a weapon. Simpson concluded that Hoerchner had badgered Hill to make a similar charge "for the women of America" to ward off "the end of pro-choice America," just as Hatch had come to believe that "feminist lawyers and feminist special interest groups" had put words in Hill's mouth. My own guess is that Hill didn't want Thomas on the Court because she also strongly opposed his anti-affirmative-action views.[51] Years later, in what Simpson recalls as a cordial and fascinating phone conversation, Hill told him that she had felt "manipulated" by pro-choice feminists.[52]

But even assuming that Hill's allegations were true (which, along with Simpson and Hatch, I do not), do not such alleged actions seem gross but trivial, worthy of a weary roll of the eyes rather than a Senate hearing—especially when compared not just with George H.W. Bush's debauched successor but also with more recent verified revelations of bosses routinely grabbing their employees' private parts, forcibly kissing them, using their power over their careers to coerce them to have sex of various kinds with them, savagely beating them as purported sexual "role playing," even raping them? All women ought to be able to go to work without being fondled or backed into a corner to be relentlessly propositioned day after day. But must they never hear an off-color comment or dirty joke? Would that not be an offense against good taste or good manners rather than the law? As Senator Hatch accurately told two *Washington Post* reporters, even if "Anita Hill was right, was telling the truth, the most you could say is

[Thomas] talked dirty to her. He didn't try to seduce her. He didn't touch her. He didn't indicate impropriety."[53]

————

MANY VIEWERS glued to the televised hearings began to rethink Hill's overall credibility after Thomas started his rebuttal. Public opinion surged in his favor, with 55 percent of respondents to a *Washington Post*–ABC poll incredulous, compared with 34 percent who believed her.[54] When the full Senate voted on Tuesday evening, October 15, the vote was a narrow 52–48 to confirm.

"Whoop-dee-damn-doo," said Thomas from the bathtub, when his wife told him the news.

He joined the Supreme Court on November 1, 1991.

CHAPTER THREE

Who Killed
the Constitution?

The bench to which he had ascended, he quickly realized, was interpreting a very different Constitution from the one that the framers had written in 1787, that the first Congress had amended by the Bill of Rights, and that the Reconstruction-era Thirteenth, Fourteenth, and Fifteenth Amendments, plus the 1920 Nineteenth Amendment, had perfected. It was a far cry from the Constitution that civics classes taught in the days when such classes still were taught. How that transformation occurred is a vital, little-known, and not always uplifting tale. For Thomas, wrestling with that change has been at the core of his career as a justice, and we can't understand his crusade without tracing how the constitutional tangle came about.

It developed in three distinct stages. The most heartbreaking part of the history, for Thomas, is its least-known first chapter, in which the very Court on which he now sits crippled the Civil War amendments meant to enfranchise fully his own people. Hundreds of thousands of Union soldiers had gone off to war singing the "Battle Hymn of the Republic," with its vow to make men free; and Lincoln's Emancipation Proclamation and the Thirteenth Amendment had ended slavery, while the Fourteenth Amendment aimed to clothe black Americans with all the rights enumerated by the Bill of Rights and the Fifteenth to guarantee their right to vote. But Reconstruction didn't go as planned. It got derailed and defeated, in as ugly a fashion as human malice can contrive, with the Supreme Court delivering the coup de grace.

Here's the backstory to the Court's two momentous, disgraceful decisions—a bit long, but truly gripping. It starts with John Wilkes Booth's assassination of President Lincoln on April 15, 1865, four days after the 26-year-old fanatic had heard the president speak of giving the vote at least to specially deserving blacks. "That means nigger citizenship," Booth snarled. "That is the last speech he will ever make."[1] Andrew Johnson, a Tennessee ex-slave-owning senator chosen as vice president as a gesture of reconciliation to the South, also proved to be no with-malice-toward-none man upon his succession to the presidency. "I am for a *white* Mans Government," he assured a fellow Tennessean, and he met a Tennessee official's plea to consider "establishing schools and organizing industries" for freedmen with frigid indifference. Usurping Congress's prerogative, he decreed that the rebel Confederate states could reconstitute their governments and elect such legislators as they wished.

Southerners, emboldened by Johnson's broad hint that Reconstruction really meant restoration of the old regime, filled their new legislatures with ex-Confederate officers and officials, whose treason Johnson had pardoned wholesale. Six such bodies promptly enacted black codes, barring freedmen from owning guns or knives, marrying whites, or exercising free speech. The codes empowered local officials to label freed blacks "vagrants" or "paupers" and bid them out as laborers. So much for liberty.[2]

And so much for life. In May 1866, white mobs in Memphis, including many police and firemen, slaughtered 48 blacks and burned down every single black school and church, plus many black homes. In July, New Orleans police murdered 38 blacks and wounded 146. *The Nation* marveled over "the coolness with which [President Johnson] refrained from expressing one word of honest indignation at the slaughter."[3]

But indignation flamed from the new Congress that convened in March 1867. It nullified Johnson's vetoes of four 1866 Civil Rights Acts that dissolved the self-reconstituted Southern state governments, and it put the South under the rule of five military commandants, who created voter registries that excluded former Confederates and included freedmen. Result: 1.3 million registered Southern voters, 54 percent of them black. Johnson responded by replacing the pro-civil-rights military commandants in 1867 with anti-black ones and by trying to sideline their boss, War Secretary Edward Stanton—and Congress impeached him early in 1868 for this violation of the (questionably constitutional) Tenure of Office Act. Though the Senate failed to convict, Johnson's power was shorn for the rest of his term. As his presidency wound down in the summer of 1868, Congress readmitted to the Union seven of the ten Confederate states that accepted its terms, and had elected significant minorities of black legislators—though it ejected Georgia once again in 1869 for expelling its black lawmakers.[4]

———

SUCCEEDING JOHNSON was Ulysses S. Grant, the brilliant general who had won the Civil War and received Robert E. Lee's surrender at Appomattox with sterling with-malice-toward-none magnanimity, allowing the defeated general and his men to depart with their banners, weapons, and horses—to plow their fields and shoot their crows, as Lincoln said. During the war, as his friendship with the president deepened, Grant had come to share Lincoln's growing conviction that the struggle's ultimate object, even beyond preserving the Union, was freeing the slaves, and he embarked upon his own presidency with the view that the protection of black voting rights—enshrined in the Fifteenth Amendment, ratified a month before his March 1869 inauguration—was "a measure of grander importance than any other one...from the foundation of our government to the present day."[5]

But despite his 58 percent popular-vote victory in the 1868 election, he sensed that his pro-civil-rights radical Republican party was losing steam. It had lost congressional seats, its old stalwarts were dying off, and younger Northerners—as Grant could divine from his loss in New York City and State by huge margins—didn't support keeping troops in the South. Even fervent abolitionists, viewing blacks as equal in rights but inferior socially and culturally, didn't relish having freedmen come north to live beside them but wanted them to stay down south. Indeed, Illinois residents even sent a train carrying black war refugees back where it came from, and Northern pressure halted the army's program of sending displaced blacks north.[6]

Grant also knew that Senator Adelbert Ames of Mississippi was right to say that the "country makes a sad and grievous mistake when it supposes that the evils of slavery and rebellion vanished on that day of surrender at Appomattox Court House." The war hadn't really ended but rather had changed in character. As a Confederate had promised, "Instead of organized armies we shall have bands of assassins everywhere in the field, and the stiletto and the torch will take the place of the sword and the musket." These revanchist militias, mostly Confederate army veterans, loosed a guerilla reign of terror upon freedmen, a long coda to the Civil War, starting with threats and moving on to arson, beating, rape, murder, lynching, and massacre, of which the 1866 Memphis and New Orleans pogroms were just the beginning. Southern blacks lived in a dragon-ridden nightmare, in which any rustle in the woods could be a banditti bent on terrorism and murder, as General Philip Sheridan told the secretary of war, and behind every tree could be a mounted marauder of the White League, the White Line, the Knights of the White Camelia, or the Ku Klux Klan, cocking a shotgun.[7]

———

THE TERRORISTS had three principal goals, and they ruthlessly gained all of them. They wanted to shut down black schools and chase away their teachers, calico-clad New England schoolmarms who began flooding the South as the war ended. In setting up nearly a thousand schools almost overnight, they for the first time ever established "between the white and black of this country a contact on terms of essential social equality and mutual respect," wrote W.E.B. Du Bois.[8] But Confederate diehards didn't want blacks educated enough to advance themselves and become equals, and they loathed being taxed for black schools. So the opportunity passed to prepare for the rapidly modernizing nineteenth century the vast majority of people whom, under slavery, it had been a crime so much as to teach to read, and who in many cases had never seen the world more than a mile or two from the plantation where they were born and held in bondage. So horrified by the obvious spiritual and intellectual, as well as physical, violence done to slaves was English novelist Charles Dickens when he had a glimpse of slavery during his 1842 American tour, so vehemently did he not want to see again "the darkness—not of skin, but mind—which meets the stranger's eye at every turn; the brutalizing and blotting out of all the fairer characters traced by Nature's hand," that he instantly changed his long-planned itinerary so as not to see another slave state.[9] More than a tragic missed opportunity, entailing decades of suffering, this aspect of what may be called Deconstruction was a crime against humanity.

The banditti also wanted to force freedmen back into the cotton fields—another reason for withholding from them the means of rising in the world. The post-slavery system gave them a share of the crops they grew on such disadvantageous terms as to amount to serfdom under their former masters, as "subject to their will as then," one petition from former slaves complained, so that it "is not the condition of really freemen."[10] But the ruined South—the war had cost it $13.6 billion— wanted its cotton, its only source of income and still the nation's major export commodity, amounting to nearly two-thirds of U.S. exports by 1889 and three-quarters of the world's supply.[11]

The serfdom was as much a cultural as an economic matter. "Slavery is so strong that it could exist, not only without law, but even against law," Frederick Douglass lamented. "Customs, manners, morals, religion, are all on its side everywhere in the South." Poet Walt Whitman, a Civil War hospital volunteer who later interviewed pardon-seeking

Confederates, remarked that "in any other country on the globe, the whole batch of Confederate leaders would have had their heads cut off."[12] Certainly that would have been the quickest solution to the cultural challenge—though the Stalinist "No man, no problem" formula thankfully lies outside the American tradition. President Grant's conclusion was milder but not mild. "Looking back over the whole policy of reconstruction, it seems to me that the wisest thing would have been to have continued for some time the military rule," he mused during his post-presidential world tour. "That was our right as a conqueror, and it was a mild penalty for the stupendous crime of treason." Additionally, "it would have been just ... to the negro who wanted his freedom." But "it was not in accordance with our institutions," and Americans would not permit it.[13]

———

THIRD, THE KKK and its ilk aimed to terrify blacks from voting and thus nullify their political power. What White Liners did in Colfax, Louisiana, on Easter Sunday 1873, the most inhuman example of terrorist tactics to that end, produced one of the Supreme Court decisions at issue here. Both Republicans and Democrats claimed victory in the state's 1872 gubernatorial election, until federal troops determined that the Republican had won. But that winner dithered before appointing black Republicans as sheriff and other officers of Grant County, emboldening white Democrats to claim the offices as theirs, by right of previous appointment. To safeguard their just claim, black Republicans occupied the courthouse in the hamlet of Colfax, the county seat.[14]

As news spread of mounted White Liners flooding daily into the swampy woods around Colfax, frightened blacks crowded into the courthouse for sanctuary. On Sunday, April 13, some 300 whites with rifles and a cannon surrounded 400 or 500 blacks packed into the courthouse. That afternoon, after giving the women and children half an hour to escape, the whites opened fire. Some of the blacks tried to flee by an unguarded route, but horsemen ran them down and shot them. Those remaining returned fire from the courthouse windows, under a rain of bullets and a relentless cannonade. Late that afternoon, the whites promised a black prisoner they *might* let him live if he would walk to the courthouse and torch it with flaming oily rags atop a fishing pole. In the ensuing inferno, the blacks waved flags of surrender and ran out, or jumped out of windows, their clothes aflame. The whites shot them down like dogs and mutilated their bodies.[15]

That night, drunken white youths killed the remaining prisoners in groups. "Many were shot in the back at the head or neck; one man still lay with his hands clasped in supplication; the face of another was completely flattened by blows from a gun," recounted a New Orleans police colonel, who later arrived on the scene. "Many of them had their brains literally blown out." His men buried 54 of the perhaps 150 murdered men, many of the rest left to rot in the swamp or be eaten by dogs and vultures.[16] An historical marker erected on the site in 1950 commemorates what historians call the Colfax Massacre as the "Colfax Riot"—supposedly the fault of blacks—which "marked the end of carpetbag misrule in the South."

———

WAS NO ONE PUNISHED for this atrocity? Enter the Supreme Court, and the answer is—No. No one.

The Court set the stage for this abdication the day after the massacre—April 14, 1873—when it handed down its decision in the *Slaughter-House Cases*, which began its shredding of the Fourteenth Amendment's key protections of the civil rights of Southern blacks, even while forcefully declaring that the amendment's "main purpose was to establish the citizenship of the negro," which the Court's 1857 *Dred Scott* v. *Sandiford* decision had categorically denied. Justice Samuel Freeman Miller, writing for the majority, acknowledged that the case's importance went far beyond the particular grievances of the plaintiffs in the three cases before it—New Orleans–area butchers who claimed that Louisiana violated their Fourteenth Amendment right to earn a living by forcing them to move into a single facility, to confine their trade's pollution to one area. The nation, said Miller, anxiously wanted to know just how the Court would construe the Fourteenth Amendment, ratified in 1868. And he proceeded to give an answer as strange as any the Court has ever issued, especially considering that he was an abolitionist appointed by Lincoln.

Yes, the Fourteenth Amendment had indeed extended the privileges and immunities of citizenship to freedmen. But, he cautioned, never forget that the amendment made black Americans citizens both of the United States and also of the state where they resided, and the privileges and immunities of state citizenship were different from those of national citizenship—and were all those that had to do with the vital matters of life, liberty, property, and the pursuit of happiness. Federal privileges and immunities? They included, Miller held, such privileges as the right not to be subject to bills of attainder or ex post facto laws, to travel on interstate waterways, and to petition the federal government for redress of grievances.

No wonder three of Miller's brethren strenuously dissented. The question before the Court, wrote Lincoln appointee Stephen Johnson Field for the dissenters, is "of the gravest importance...to the whole country. It is nothing less than the question whether the recent amendments to the Federal Constitution protect the citizens of the United States against the deprivation of their common rights by State legislation. In my judgment, the fourteenth amendment does afford such protection, and was so intended by the Congress which framed and the States which adopted it." In other words, the Fourteenth Amendment does indeed extend the protections of the Bill of Rights from state infringement.

A separate dissent by Justice Noah Swayne explains one consideration that may have pushed the majority toward so bizarre a conclusion. They might have worried that the Fourteenth Amendment too greatly altered the federalist balance of power between the states and the central government that the framers had poised. The Civil War, Swayne noted, dispelled the framers' fear of an overly powerful central government. "The public mind became satisfied that there was less danger of tyranny in the head than of anarchy and tyranny in the members," he wrote. "The construction adopted by the majority of my brethren . . . turns, as it were, what was meant for bread into a stone. By the Constitution as it stood before the war, ample protection was given against oppression by the Union, but little was given against wrong and oppression by the States. That want was intended to be supplied by this amendment."[17]

Clarence Thomas objects no less strenuously, though even more vividly, to Justice Miller's opinion. "We all agree *Slaughter-House* is wrongly decided. It has had a profound effect on this country," he said in 2016, to "guarantee citizenship to people—the privileges or immunities of citizenship that cannot be impinged upon—and then you read it out of the Constitution or you trivialize it or you minimize it."

He offered a lighthearted analogy. "If I said to you, 'You're a member of my club. You have all the privileges or immunities of membership in this club.' Then I rewrite the privileges or immunities to mean you get to ride the elevator once a week—and that's it. You'd say, 'Boy, that's a heck of a membership. Everybody else is swimming, and they're in the gym, or they're in the sauna, and I just get to ride the elevator once!' That's the way I feel about the Privileges or Immunities Clause." And then he turned deadly serious. "I have a personal interest in this. I lived under segregation," he said. The Fourteenth Amendment's privileges or immunities clause is "not just a theory. It is what makes it all work. It was a way to perfect a blemish on this country's history. That is the blemish of slavery. It was the big contradiction, and we fought a war over it."[18]

———

INVOKING *SLAUGHTER-HOUSE* as a precedent, the Court unanimously let Colfax Massacre perpetrators get off scot-free in *United States* v. *Cruikshank*, a decision so tendentious that it still oozes slime a century and a half later. No white Louisiana jury would convict whites of killing blacks, so federal prosecutors indicted a handful of White Liners for violating the 1870 Enforcement Act, one of a series of laws Congress passed to say *we really mean the Fourteenth and Fifteenth Amendments*! So while the Fourteenth Amendment forbids states from abridging the privileges or immunities of citizens of the United States, the Enforcement Act makes it a crime for individuals to conspire to prevent or punish a citizen for exercising those rights. Three terrorists convicted under this law appealed to the Supreme Court.

Hang on! wrote Chief Justice Morrison Waite for the Court in *Cruikshank* in March 1876. The Constitution and Bill of Rights did not *give* citizens the rights the document mentions. These are the unalienable rights given man by the Creator, not by the United States. The Constitution merely forbids Congress from *interfering with* those rights. So because such rights as peaceful assembly or bearing arms are not privileges or immunities bestowed by U.S. citizenship, the Fourteenth Amendment has no bearing on whether a state can interfere with them. As for the amendment's ban on a *state* depriving any citizen of life, liberty, or property without due process of law, or depriving him of the equal protection of the laws: well, that has nothing to do with the *individual* defendants here—even though of course the Enforcement Act most emphatically does make it a crime for individuals to conspire to do just that.

Twisting the knife still further, the chief justice notes that an earlier Court decision had found that the Fifteenth Amendment does not make the right to vote "a necessary attribute of national citizenship." It only forbids "discrimination in the exercise of the elective franchise on account of race, color, or previous condition of servitude."[19] So the Southern states were freed to cook up their various "nondiscriminatory" ploys to deny blacks the vote.

The decision helped embolden Southern Democrats to enact Jim Crow laws, the black codes redux. From *Cruickshank* it took but a short step to *Plessy v. Ferguson*, the infamous 1896 decision in which the Supreme Court obliterated still more of the rights that the Fourteenth Amendment had given blacks by allowing the Southern states to legislate segregated transportation and schools and to outlaw interracial marriage. So much for Abraham Lincoln's dream of finishing the work the Civil War had begun and binding up the nation's wounds with malice toward none and charity for all.

Thus did the Court dishonor the sacrifice of the hundreds of thousands—almost a whole generation—who had died to make men free. And thus did it overturn the will of the people, through their elected representatives, to change the Constitution lawfully and to accomplish through the Fourteenth Amendment what the framers deeply believed but could not themselves bring to pass: to embody in the fundamental law of the land the founding proposition that all men are created equal in rights. The 1868 Congress, made up of representatives of the victor states, would not readmit representatives of the treasonous states unless their legislatures ratified the Fourteenth Amendment. They intended to use their costly victory in a murderously bloody war to give the central government enough strength to force the Southern states to do what the framers lacked the political might to bring to pass. But the Supreme Court helped make a mockery of all that Herculean effort.

———

THE NEXT STAGE in the century-long transformation of the Constitution rested on not even a pretense of constitutionality. The keynote of the 1787 Constitution is its prudent restraint. The framers learned from hard Revolutionary War experience that their new nation needed a more powerful central government than the Articles of Confederation authorized. But they bestowed the requisite powers with a trembling hand, knowing that the men who would exercise them were not angels but humans, as fallible as all other men and usually more so, since overweening ambition and self-interest, not patriotism, are the standard spurs to seeking office. Recognizing that electing your officials doesn't ensure that they won't become as tyrannical as the hereditary monarchs the colonists had fled—there can be, they said, such a thing as an "elective despotism," usurping the free, republican *self*-government they sought—the framers hemmed in and divided government authority, giving Congress only 19 specific powers that mostly concerned raising taxes, regulating commerce, coining money, spending it on "the common Defence and general Welfare of the United States" (meaning keeping the country safe), building post offices and post roads (but not turnpikes and canals), regulating the armed forces, and making laws necessary and proper to carry out these limited functions. Constitution architect James Madison, always at the vortex of the fierce disputes over what measures these enumerated powers implied as necessary and proper, concluded—after serving for a quarter century as a congressman, secretary of state, and president—that the bedrock constitutional principle was simply to ensure that America does not "convert a limited into an unlimited Govt."[20]

But President Woodrow Wilson, who set in motion this second phase of constitutional change, viewed these great men and their remarkable work with condescension. In his eyes, they were bewigged relics of a vanished age unconnected with modernity, and their plan of a limited government of strictly enumerated powers, hedged with checks and balances, was equally obsolete in the new age of science and statistics, professionalism and progress. Our laws, he said, have not kept up with the vast changes that have occurred in our economic and political circumstances. And no wonder, for they were made under a Constitution modeled on the Newtonian universe, its checks and balances mirroring the centrifugal and centripetal forces that keep the planets forever moving in their spheres like a vast machine. "The trouble with the theory is that government is not a machine, but a living thing. It falls, not under the theory of the universe, but under the theory of organic life. It is accountable to Darwin, not to Newton," Wilson asserted. "No living thing can have its organs offset against each other, as checks, and live.... Living political constitutions must be Darwinian in structure and practice. Society is a living organism and must obey the laws of life, not of mechanics; it must develop."[21] Can't get much more up-to-date and scientific than evolution.

"The chief instrumentality by which the law of the Constitution has been extended to cover the facts of national development has of course been judicial interpretations,—the decisions of courts," wrote Wilson, Virginia-born and Princeton-educated like Madison but in every other respect his polar opposite. "The process of formal amendment of the Constitution was made so difficult by the...Constitution itself that it has seldom been feasible to use it." So the doughty courts have stepped in and taken over the "whole business of adaptation...with open minds, sometimes even with boldness and a touch of audacity," becoming "more liberal, not to say more lax, in their interpretation than they otherwise would have been." Wilson's living Constitution—it was he who popularized the phrase—meant that the Supreme Court would make up the laws as it went along. Of course, "if the policy of the government upon vital questions, affecting the whole people, is to be irrevocably fixed by decisions of the Supreme Court," as Lincoln warned in his First Inaugural Address almost half a century earlier (and as Clarence Thomas perceives today), "the people will have ceased to be their own rulers."[22]

But Wilson cared less about using the Court as a permanent constitutional convention than making it a force to clear away the Constitution's restraints and limitations, so that the nation could move to a post-political "upland where the air is fresher, where the whole talk of mere politicians is stilled."[23] In his view, "The period of constitution-making is passed now. We have reached a new territory in which we need new guides, the vast territory of *administration*." In our modern age, "The functions of government are in a very real sense independent of legislation, and even constitutions.... Administration cannot wait upon legislation, but must be given leave, or take it, to proceed without specific warrant in giving effect to the characteristic life of the State."[24]

Instead of the people's elected representatives making laws under constitutional limits, expert bureaucrats with advanced degrees, working with "disinterested ambition" in non-political, independent administrative agencies like the Interstate Commerce Commission, formed in 1887, or the Federal Trade Commission, founded during Wilson's presidency, would smoothly institute measures that economics and social science, continually advancing, would reveal as the common good. After all, "an intelligent nation cannot be led or ruled save by thoroughly trained and completely-educated men. Only comprehensive information and entire mastery of principles and details can qualify for command." There is nothing of democratic self-government in the "command" of this newly hatched, elitist administrative state, of course. But ultimately Wilson didn't subscribe to the fundamental American proposition. "No doubt a great deal of nonsense has been talked about the inalienable rights of the individual, and a great deal that was mere vague sentiment and pleasing speculation has been put forward as fundamental principle," he wrote. "The rights of man are very easy to discourse of,...but they are infinitely hard to translate into practice. Such theories are never 'law.'... Only that is 'law' which can be executed."[25]

A political science professor and Princeton University president before his election as U.S. president, Wilson had fallen under the spell of a quite different political tradition from American republicanism. He had learned German to read philosopher G.W.F. Hegel and his followers, and he embraced their concept of the *Rechtsstaat*, whose ideology replaces "the contract theory of the origin of the state" with the idea that the function of the state is not to protect individual rights but rather to take "general care for the interests of the community," as the University of Chicago's hugely influential political science chairman Charles Merriam had put it in 1903. This was the ideology of the European enlightened despots of the eighteenth century, especially Prussia's Frederick the Great, who ruled through a meritocratic class of efficient, educated, benevolent bureaucrats, who, more than ordinary citizens, could divine the spirit of the times and knew which way the arc of history bent, so they could speed it along in the right direction. Though this was absolutism with a beautifully humanistic face, it remained absolutism. However perilous, this theory held in thrall almost all of American academic political science at the time, from Columbia University to the Institute for Government Research (later renamed the Brookings Institution). Its chairman, Johns Hopkins president Frank Goodnow, argued that the individual's rights are "conferred upon him" by his society, so that "[s]ocial expedience, rather than natural right, is thus to determine the sphere of individual freedom of action." That was in 1916; so don't think universities became threats to freedom only in our day.[26]

———

WILSON CONCOCTED and legitimized the magic elixir of judicial constitution-making and rule by administrative agencies, but Franklin D. Roosevelt employed it like an alchemist to transmute the American political system into a full-blown administrative state that resembled George III's system of rulers and subjects as much as it did George Washington's government. The magnitude of the Great Depression, Roosevelt thought, required the federal government to seize control of the entire U.S. economy. Only national rather than state or free-market solutions, he believed, could nurse it back to health. The Supreme Court batted down his first attempts to use the Commerce Clause—the power that Article I, Section 8 of the Constitution gives Congress to regulate interstate commerce—to regulate *all* commerce, including commerce that never crosses a state line. In 1935, for example, the Court struck down a law mandating retirement plans for railway workers, noting that, even though railways participate in interstate transportation, their workers' pension plans do not.[27] That same year, the Court declared that Congress had no power, via the National Industrial Recovery Act, to set the wages and hours of Brooklyn poultry workers or to regulate how they sell chickens, since neither the workers nor the chickens leave New York State.[28] Nor, said the Court the following year, could Congress set up commissions to decree coal prices or miners' working conditions. Yes, strikes interrupt production, affect prices nationwide, and thus affect interstate commerce, but they and the conditions that cause them "are local evils over which the federal government has no legislative control."[29]

But once Roosevelt's plan for a constitutional amendment to curb the Court's power scared Justice Owen Roberts into changing his judicial spots, the Nine began to toe the New Deal line. Just as FDR's

Progressive cousin Theodore Roosevelt had blamed the global financial instability preceding the Panic of 1907 on giant corporations—often led, said TR, by "malefactors of great wealth"—Franklin Roosevelt also saw big business as a threat to ordinary individuals, whom only big government could protect. "We have earned the hatred of entrenched greed," the president accusingly said of corporate America in his 1936 State of the Union speech. "Give them their way and they will take the course of every autocracy of the past—power for themselves, enslavement for the public."

On cue, in its 1937 *Jones & Laughlin* decision, the Court upheld the National Labor Relations Act, whose "major function," according to Richard Epstein, "was to prop up union monopolies in labor relations." To reach its decision, the Court noted that the big steel company had "far-flung activities" across the nation, so that "industrial strife" in any one of them "would have a most serious effect upon interstate commerce.... [I]t is idle to say that the effect would be indirect or remote. It is obvious that it would be immediate, and might be catastrophic." Hence J&L's intrastate activities "have such a close and intimate relation to interstate commerce as to make the presence of industrial strife a matter of the most urgent national concern. When industries organize themselves on a national scale, making their relation to interstate commerce the dominant factor in their activities, how can it be maintained that their industrial labor relations constitute a forbidden field into which Congress may not enter when it is necessary to protect interstate commerce from the paralyzing consequences of industrial war?"[30] Further federalizing local economic activity, the Court declared in its 1941 *Darby* decision, with all the audacity Woodrow Wilson could have wanted, that *of course* the Fair Labor Standards Act could force firms not engaged in interstate commerce to observe national wage and hour standards, even though they were following the standards of their home states, and *of course* the FLSA could bar from interstate commerce any product it defined as "produced under substandard labor conditions."[31]

The logical but lunatic capstone to this line of reasoning was the Court's 1942 *Wickard* v. *Filburn* decision. In accordance with FDR and his brain trust's incorrect belief that the Depression stemmed from a crisis of deflationary overproduction, the Agricultural Adjustment Act, purportedly based on Congress's Commerce Clause power, directed the Department of Agriculture to establish a crop quota system, allocating so much production to each state, which in turn would prescribe the permitted output for each farm. For exceeding his wheat allotment, Ohio farmer Roscoe Filburn was fined $117.11, or 49 cents per each bushel of excess production. But here's the rub: agriculture isn't commerce, as the founders understood it, and not only did Filburn's grain not enter into interstate commerce, but it didn't even enter into in-state commerce, since he fed it to his own cows. But even if the grain "is never marketed," the Court wrote in true *Alice in Wonderland* style, "it supplied the need of the man who grew it which would otherwise be reflected by purchases in the open market. Home-grown wheat in this sense competes with wheat in commerce. The stimulation of commerce is a use of the regulatory function quite as definitely as prohibitions or restrictions thereon." Even if Filburn's "activity be local and though it may not be regarded as commerce," the Court ruled, "it may still, whatever its nature, be reached by Congress if it exerts a substantial economic effect on interstate commerce."[32] The lengths to which free people will go to evade central planners' price controls!

———

THE NEW DEAL didn't transform the Constitution only by institutionalizing nine unelected judges with lifetime tenure as a permanent constitutional convention, turning Woodrow Wilson's theory into hard reality. It also allowed Congress to create, at the president's request and with the blessing of the Court, an unprecedented regulatory state, made up of a constellation of administrative agencies—from the Federal Housing Administration and the Federal Communications Commission to the National Labor Relations Board and the Securities and Exchange Commission—that make rules, enforce them, and adjudicate transgressions of them. "The practice of creating independent regulatory commissions, who perform administrative work in addition to judicial work," Roosevelt himself admitted, "threatens to develop a 'fourth branch' of Government for which there is no sanction in the Constitution."[33]

That is an understatement, not just about the New Deal agencies but also about those created by the regulation-crazed Great Society— the Environmental Protection Agency, for instance, or the Occupational Safety and Health Administration, or the Consumer Product Safety Commission—and the agencies created under the Dodd-Frank Act and the Affordable Care Act passed under President Barack Obama, who, like professor-president Woodrow Wilson, was certain he knew better than the American people which way the arc of the moral universe bends.[34]

It's hard to count the ways in which the administrative or regulatory state overturns, abolishes, and usurps the Constitution. The Constitution lodges *all* legislative power in Congress, which therefore cannot delegate its lawmaking function elsewhere. So it's forbidden for Congress to pass a law creating an independent or executive-branch agency that writes rules legally binding on citizens—for example, to set up an agency charged with making a clean environment and then to let it make rules with the force of law to accomplish that end as it sees fit. As the American Revolution's tutelary philosopher, John Locke, had pronounced, the legislative branch has the authority "only to make laws, and not to make legislators"—but that's just what Congress has done in creating administrative-agency rule makers. And if Congress can't delegate the legislative power that the Constitution gives it, it certainly cannot delegate power that the Constitution doesn't give it, such as the power to hand out selective exemptions from its laws, as agencies do when they grant waivers.[35]

In addition, these are legislators who execute the rules they decree and adjudicate and punish infringements of them, an egregious violation of the "separation-of-powers doctrine under the Constitution" that "dispens[es] with our principal safeguard against autocracy in government," the American Bar Association warned in 1936, as the administrative state was taking shape. "We should not have some 73 midget courts in Washington, most of them exercising legislative and executive powers. A man should not be judge in his own case and the combination of prosecutor and judge in these tribunals must be relentlessly exposed and combatted"—the more so because judicial power is as undelegatable as legislative power, and furthermore the Constitution lodges all of it in the judicial branch. So while administrative judges may look "just like real judges," says Philip Hamburger, they are no such thing—and not only because Article III of the Constitution makes it impossible for them to be so but also because, unlike real judges, their sole duty, rather than using their independent and expert judgment to carry out the law of the land, is to carry out the policy of their agency, as set and overseen by their department chief or the relevant cabinet secretary who in turn oversees them. As Chief Justice William Howard Taft pronounced, an administrative tribunal is "miscalled a court."[36]

Making matters worse, as even New Deal Democratic congressman Emanuel Celler ruefully noted, many of the "experts" staffing these agencies are "mere 'whipper-snappers'—young students just out of law school—who apparently are given undue authority in originating, if not effectuating, final decisions."[37] The rules they make often don't even bear the imprimatur of the Senate-confirmed officer who nominally oversees them.[38] And, though these are supposed to be executive-branch agencies, it's not always clear under whose authority they operate. Some, like the Securities and Exchange Commission or the Consumer Product Safety Commission, are supposedly independent—a constitutional non sequitur. As for the Federal Trade Commission, the Supreme Court declared it more a judicial and legislative agency than an executive-branch one, another non sequitur.[39]

Worst of all, the regulatory agencies may presume anyone they charge to be guilty unless he proves his innocence, and he has but limited standing and scope to appeal the agency's decision to a real court, effectively "making the commission's decisions on fact final and conclusive," the ABA objected. "This sets the wheels of government moving in reverse gear; the servant becomes the master, and the right to earn a living becomes subject to the servant's whim and caprice as he professes to apply some vague and variable statutory standard." Little wonder that one congressman warned that "government by committees, boards, bureaus, and commissions will, if unchecked and uncontrolled, destroy the republican conception of government"—or that a senator deemed one of the agencies a "star chamber," the arbitrary, juryless court of Stuart despotism, where due process (as first laid out in Magna Carta over 800 years ago and reiterated in the U.S. Constitution's Fifth Amendment) had no place.[40] That's the trouble with the enlightened despotism Woodrow Wilson admired: the despotism outlasts the enlightenment—as the founders could have told him.

———

WHAT WOULD Thomas Jefferson—who complained in the Declaration of Independence that George III had "erected a Multitude of new Offices, and sent hither Swarms of Officers to harrass our People, and eat out their Substance"—have to say about a 2.6 million-person federal bureaucracy, with salaries 16 percent higher and employee benefits 48 percent higher than its private-sector counterparts, so that the bedroom communities surrounding Washington are now the richest neighborhoods in the nation whose taxes support them? What would George Washington—whom the Senate declared didn't need its approval to dismiss Senate-confirmed executive-branch officers, since he alone was responsible to the voters for their actions—have to say about the civil service rules and union protections that make the whippersnappers so difficult, and often impossible, to fire? Even Franklin Roosevelt thought bureaucrat unions an absurdity.[41]

For the mountain of money they extract from taxpayers, how much of the expertise, efficiency, and nonpartisan disinterestedness that Woodrow Wilson promised do these bureaucratic hordes provide? Expertise? In 2015, Environmental Protection Agency "experts" fecklessly stood by as workers under their supervision accidentally dumped 3 million gallons of toxic wastewater into the Colorado River, and the agency vouchsafed not a word of warning to downstream Colorado and New Mexico officials for an entire day before the poisonous, fluorescent-orange flood hit them. Over at Veterans Affairs, those who've fought for their country die in droves while waiting for medical care. But what's the problem? asked the then agency head blithely in 2016. After all, at ever-popular Disneyland, "do they measure the number of hours you wait in line?" Or how about the cyber experts at the Office of Personnel Management, who in 2015 failed to stop Chinese hackers from stealing millions of government employee files, fingerprints, and background checks, containing such details as financial transactions, Social Security numbers, substance abuse, psychiatric history, or sexual shenanigans?

Efficiency? Can-do America, which built the Empire State Building in 11 months and ramped up airplane production during World War II from 2,000 in 1939 to nearly 100,000 in 1944, now takes years of bureaucratic EPA busywork to repair a bridge or lay a pipeline, and who knows how many businesses never expand or even start because the maze of government regulation is too daunting and costly to navigate? Where is the Food and Drug Administration as counterfeit medicines and medical supplies from China infiltrate our hospitals? As for the infamously dysfunctional Transportation Security Administration, its Keystone Kops' chronic inability to spot journalists carrying banned weapons onto airplanes, while they are too busy fondling travelers' private parts or undressing grannies, is a standing national joke—on us.

Where were the Securities and Exchange Commission, the Federal Reserve, the Office of Thrift Supervision, and the Office of Federal Housing Enterprise Oversight as the mortgage bubble burst in 2008, nearly taking the whole financial system with it and producing the worst economic bust since the Great Depression? Moreover, from the establishment of the first administrative agency—the Interstate Commerce Commission in 1887, essentially designed to create shared railroad cartels—these agencies have been key instruments of crony capitalism, which today often takes the form of senators and congressmen pressuring agencies for rule changes or waivers to benefit their contributors, usually at the expense of their competitors as well as the public, as the author of the 2016 *Confessions of Congressman X* complains of his fellow legislative "puppets." Little wonder that today's Americans think that such people don't represent them. Pollsters report that trust in government is at its lowest level ever, with only 18 percent expecting government to do the right thing, according to a 2017 Pew poll.[42]

Impartially and disinterestedly non-political? Federal bureaucrats have always leaned to the political Left, "idealistic" and "progressive," as they say of themselves by way of praise, for they claim to know the direction of history as well as their early twentieth-century Progressive movement forebears. But what should we say about the Internal Revenue Service's deliberately partisan withholding of tax-exempt status from conservative groups for years on end—an exercise of tyrannical power in the one government function that James Madison wrote in *Federalist* 10 especially requires the utmost impartiality? How about the cool effrontery with which the IRS boss simply ignored Congress's orders, even as more than 2,000 of his enforcement agents have acquired military-grade weaponry, among 200,000 of such administrative-agency officers now similarly equipped with lethal arms, presumably for coercion of the citizens they supposedly serve? And worst of all, top officials of our Federal Bureau of Investigation and Justice Department seem to have brought to bear the incalculable power of the state to try to rig a presidential election and sabotage the winner they don't like—and they have evaded accounting for their behavior to the people's elected representatives for more than a year, as I write, citing their so-called higher loyalty. Here the administrative state morphs into something like the secret police of a banana republic or a totalitarian tyranny, flagrantly unconstitutional and un-American.

When Theodore Roosevelt, who unsuccessfully ran against Woodrow Wilson in 1912 on the Progressive Party ticket, first declared his intention to go into politics, his fellow clubmen jeered at the New York aristocrat for wanting to associate with the "saloon-keepers, horse-car conductors," and other "rough and brutal" characters running the nation's political parties. "I answered," recalled Roosevelt, "that if this were so it merely meant that the people I knew did not belong to the governing class, and that the other people did—and that I intended to be one of the governing class."[43] That's the true voice of "Progressivism" speaking. As the founders often cautioned, a self-governing republic doesn't have a governing class. Part of America's current predicament is that it now has a permanent, unelected one, unanswerable to the people. Absolutism—soft perhaps, but absolutism nonetheless—has replaced a democratic republic.

———

THE SUPREME COURT under Chief Justice Earl Warren completed the original Constitution's metamorphosis. Warren took up the gavel in 1953, in the midst of the landmark *Brown v. Board of Education* school desegregation case. The widespread public acclaim that met his opinion for a unanimous Court the following year kindled in him, his colleagues, and many of their successors for the next half century a fervent belief that the Court was properly a permanent constitutional convention, solving thorny public dilemmas with Wilsonian "boldness and a touch of audacity" when the political branches of government had reached an impasse.[44] The people's elected representatives tacitly went along, evidently relieved at not having to take responsibility for such big decisions. Abdication went hand in hand with usurpation.

Warren's *Brown* ruling, a curious mix of newfound radicalism and the conservatism that had marked his tenure as California's Republican attorney general and governor, floated utterly free from the Constitution, which gives the federal government no authority over education of any kind. Nevertheless, public education, Warren asserted, hardly universal in 1797 and still spotty when Congress framed the Fourteenth Amendment, has now become the most important and expensive function of most state and local governments, and indispensable to every child's success in life. Once a state provides universal compulsory education, the Fourteenth Amendment's demand for equal protection of the laws kicks in. Education becomes "a right which must be made available to all on equal terms," a right that the federal government must protect. Presto, a new right that has no constitutional basis!

Warren managed to slip past one constitutional barrier—the fact that the Congress that framed the Fourteenth Amendment also voted funds for the District of Columbia's segregated school system—by claiming that the randomness of public education in 1868 meant that the legislators would never have thought about the amendment's effect on it, so it's pointless to ask if they had an original intent in this matter. But a bigger obstacle loomed: the Court's 1896 *Plessy* v. *Ferguson* decision approving separate but equal facilities for blacks and whites in public accommodation. Given the Court's reverence for *stare decisis*, the doctrine that judges must respect precedent, the conservative ember in Warren made him averse simply to overrule his predecessors.

The testimony psychologist Kenneth B. Clark had offered in one of the cases under review in *Brown* provided a convenient dodge. Clark had compared the responses of black children to blond-haired, white-skinned dolls with their responses to black-haired, brown-skinned dolls. The difference between the responses of children in the segregated District of Columbia schools from those in the integrated New York City schools, he reported, proved to him that black children in segregated schools had lower self-esteem than those in integrated schools. The chief justice approvingly quoted the lower court's summary of this research: "'Segregation with the sanction of law, therefore, has a tendency to [retard] the educational and mental development of negro children and to deprive them of some of the benefits they would receive in a racial[ly] integrated school system.'" Consequently, Warren ruled, "We conclude that, in the field of public education, the doctrine of 'separate but equal' has no place. Separate educational facilities are inherently unequal." It was a deft way of sidestepping *Plessy* in the special case of education without actually overruling the 1896 decision, and thus remaining faithful to *stare decisis*.

A coda to the decision stated even more clearly its "fundamental principle that racial discrimination in public education is unconstitutional,"[45] and the 1964 Civil Rights Act reinforced and further clarified that principle, declaring that "'Desegregation' means the assignment of students to public schools and within such schools without regard to their race, color, religion, or national origin, but 'desegregation' shall not mean the assignment of children to public schools in order to overcome racial imbalance." Perhaps *Brown* prodded Congress to pass the act sooner than it otherwise would have; but pass it Congress did—and only a decade after the Court made its ruling on the basis of fanciful psychological theorizing rather than on the text of the Constitution it is charged with interpreting. In the life of a nation, ten years is not long to wait for the people's representatives to make such a decision with unquestioned legitimacy.

However—and it's a big however—the legislation set in motion a swarm of zealous "experts" in the administrative agencies, in this case the Department of Health, Education, and Welfare and the U.S. Civil Rights Commission. With their special knowledge of the spirit of the age, these whippersnappers (to use the New Deal congressman Celler's term) issued two sets of guidelines in 1965 and 1966 that turned Congress's intent upside down. Like grubs burrowing inside an apple and rotting it, they decreed that not only must local school districts stop segregating but also they must "achieve substantial integration" by assigning students based on race. One federal appeals judge bought this reversal, saying, with true Wilsonian Hegelianism, "No army is stronger than an idea whose time has come."

The Supreme Court, having got the bit between its teeth, didn't stop to parse what the act actually had said. Linking arms with the bureaucrats and the lower-court judge, in 1968 it ordered a racially mixed district where official segregation had ended, but a dual school system still existed even after kids got freedom to choose their school, to assign children to public schools precisely to overcome racial imbalance, and in 1971 it ordered school systems that formerly were officially segregated to achieve racial balance by busing, if necessary.[46] In 1973, the Court removed the question of intent in producing predominantly black and predominantly white schools, erasing its prior distinction between *de facto* and *de jure* segregation. Now racial imbalance in Northern as well as Southern school systems, even if caused by housing patterns, required "affirmative action"—and the result was a decade of nationwide busing, white flight, and the repurposing of public schools from instruments of education to instruments of racial justice.[47] Equally destructive, the doctrine of affirmative action in matters involving race (and later sex) distorted college admissions and employer hiring decisions to the point where "merit" is now deemed a racist, sexist construct that must hang its head in shame before the far nobler ideal of "diversity," an idea that would have framer Alexander Hamilton—an illegitimate orphan from the West Indies, whose merit raised him to Treasury secretary and who tried to build into the early republic the means for others to follow in his footsteps—spinning in his grave in Trinity Churchyard.[48]

———

As THE recent confirmation battle over Justice Kavanaugh's nomination to the Court shows, "the vigorous opposing views" about abortion and "the deep and seemingly absolute convictions that the subject inspires," as Justice Harry Blackmun put it in his opinion for the Court's majority in *Roe* v. *Wade*, remain just as fierce as before that Court decision supposedly settled the question.[49] But the argument about whether the policy of legalizing abortion is right or wrong is not the most important issue in thinking about this case. The real crux is whether the Court had any business to decide such a contentious matter, which the Constitution doesn't mention. I am among those who think that Blackmun's view that the law should place *some* limits on abortion while not prohibiting it entirely is correct (though I disagree on where to draw the limit), just as I think the original *Brown* ruling the correct answer to a question the Court had no warrant to decide. But, as Blackmun himself concedes, at the time he wrote, a third of the states had already liberalized their abortion laws, and public opinion was fast moving in that direction. Why preempt

the working of the popularly elected state legislatures, which were
faithfully converting the wishes of their citizens into legitimate law
and patiently untangling abortion's Gordian knot, before the Court
swooped in in 1973 and cut it with one violent stroke, which further
shredded America's self-governing constitutional order?

Moreover, although Justice (later Chief Justice) William Rehnquist's
dissent in *Roe* appropriately praised Blackmun for the "extensive historical fact and…wealth of legal scholarship" his opinion displayed—concerning what Hippocrates thought about abortion, what the common
law and the American Medical Association say—still, all this rests on
a foundation that isn't only shaky but just plain silly. It rests on the
Court's 1965 *Griswold* v. *Connecticut* ruling, which many commentators
view as the most risible Court decision of them all. Justice William O.
Douglas, writing for the majority to strike down Connecticut's contra-
ceptive ban in a case concerning a married couple, asserted that, while
the Constitution says nothing whatever on this subject, nevertheless
the "specific guarantees in the Bill of Rights have penumbras, formed
by emanations from those guarantees that help give them life and
substance"—rather like the will-o'-the-wisps that rising swamp gas
produces, ghostly shapes that seem to glow but are just gas.

"We deal with a right of privacy older than the Bill of Rights—older
than our political parties, older than our school system," Douglas va-
pored. "Marriage is a coming together for better or for worse, hopefully
enduring, and intimate to the degree of being sacred. It is an association that promotes a way of life, not causes; a harmony in living, not
political faiths;…" and so on.[50] What is certainly true, as Blackmun
acknowledges in *Roe*, is that "[t]he Constitution does not explicitly
mention any right of privacy." But it was to uphold this phantom right
of a woman no longer pregnant when he announced his opinion that
Blackmun overturned the law of Texas and any other such state laws
in the Union in *Roe* v. *Wade*. No wonder that nearly half a century later, even a *Washington Post* columnist concludes that "the way to make
abortion less contentious is to throw the matter back to the states so
that people can argue about it.… Returning the matter to the states

would give most people a law they can live with, defusing the rage that permeates politics."[51]

Busing, affirmative action, and abortion are but the three most glaring areas in which the justices have made law from the bench, with no constitutional license to do so. But as the next chapter shows, the number of such meddlings is legion, all of them subverting the idea of government by the people.

CHAPTER FOUR

Originalism in Action

O n the bench, Thomas takes precisely the opposite approach from Chief Justice Charles Evans Hughes, who notoriously quipped that "the Constitution is what the judges say it is." Under that rubric, justices too often have imposed their own policy preferences, Thomas says: "You make it up, and then you rationalize it." According to his own strictly originalist judicial credo, set forth in a 1996 speech, "The Constitution means not what the Court says it does but what the delegates at Philadelphia and at the state ratifying conventions understood it to mean.... We as a nation adopted a written Constitution precisely because it has a fixed meaning that does not change. Otherwise we would have adopted the British approach of an unwritten, evolving constitution." Consequently, "as Justice Brandeis declared in the great case of *Erie* v. *Tompkins*, there is no federal general common law. The duty of the federal courts is to interpret and enforce two bodies of positive law: the Constitution and the body of federal statutory law."[1] What the law schools teach as constitutional law is merely a compendium of opinions that might or might not be correct.

In modern times, that's a radical argument, and not just because it contradicts the Wilsonian conceit of a "living Constitution" that evolves to meet changing conditions. It also challenges the doctrine of *stare decisis*—the principle that judges should respect precedents and let them stand—which in modern times has been a handmaiden of judicial policy-making: judges tinker with the precedents until "they get what they want, and then they start yelling *stare decisis*, as though that is supposed to stop you," Thomas said in 2016. True, judges in the lower federal courts pledge to apply precedents faithfully, and many try. But Supreme Court justices, Thomas contends, "are obligated to think things through constantly, to re-examine ourselves, to go back over turf we've already plowed, to torment yourself to make sure you're right." If they discover that their predecessors were wrong, they are obliged to say so—and even to reverse the Court's earlier decisions. An iron-bound allegiance to *stare decisis*, as the Court has demonstrated more than once, can result in generations of error piled upon error. "I trust the Constitution itself. The written document is the ultimate *stare decisis*," Thomas argues. "Instead of saying *stare decisis*," he explained recently, "we should say *quo warranto*—by what authority?" Very different from Yale Law, he notes, which didn't even assign the Constitution in full.[2]

———

To SEE HOW this approach works, look at two of his opinions that seek to blunt one of constitutional demolition's key tools—the clause in the document itself that empowers Congress to "regulate commerce with foreign nations, and among the several states, and with the Indian tribes." In 1995, in *United States v. Lopez*, the Court struck down a federal law using the Commerce Clause to justify a ban on gun possession in a school zone, a matter seemingly far removed from commerce. Justice Stephen Breyer's dissent shows the kind of Rube Goldberg reasoning that too often has justified such a law: by hampering education, the forbidden activity would yield a "less-productive citizenry" with "an adverse effect on the Nation's economic well-being," he held, so Congress properly forbade it under its Commerce Clause authority.

Chief Justice William Rehnquist's majority ruling more sensibly declared that the government had exceeded its authority under the Commerce Clause, since it could not show that the forbidden activity "substantially affected" interstate commerce. But Thomas's opinion, concurring in the chief justice's judgment but not in its reasoning, warned that the long-established "substantial effects" criterion that Rehnquist invokes, "if taken to its logical extreme, would give Congress a 'police power' over all aspects of American life," from littering to marriage. Indeed, he pointed out, "when asked [in oral argument] if there were *any* limits to the Commerce Clause, the Government was at a loss for words."[3]

But there *are* limits. First, the meaning of the word "commerce" is less expansive than you might think. Founding-era dictionaries clearly define it as selling, buying, bartering, and transporting goods. Both *The Federalist* and the state ratifying conventions used the word to distinguish trade from manufacturing or agriculture, over which the Constitution gives Congress no power. Second, if the framers meant the clause to grant Congress broad authority over all matters that "substantially affect" commerce, why does Article I, Section 8, where the Commerce Clause appears, bother to enumerate such other powers as coining money or punishing counterfeiters or enacting bankruptcy laws—all of which "substantially affect" commerce, as framers James Madison and Alexander Hamilton pointed out? The Court needs to revisit its Commerce Clause jurisprudence, Thomas concluded, because "our case law has drifted far from the original understanding of the Commerce Clause" and threatens to make a reality of Madison's nightmare of a limited government becoming an unlimited one.

———

THOMAS ZEROES IN on the New Deal as the start of such misuse of the Commerce Clause to let Washington regulate the whole web of human activity. The "Court's dramatic departure in the 1930s from a century and a half of precedent" was unequivocally a "wrong turn" that marks the real start of modern illegitimate judicial lawmaking. This was not a wrong turn that the Court made happily. Up until 1936, it had resolutely resisted Congress's attempts to use the Commerce Clause as a justification for the flood of New Deal legislation. But after a frustrated Franklin Roosevelt threatened to enlarge the high bench and pack it with his partisans, Justice Owen Roberts, in the infamous switch in time that saved nine, stopped finding New Deal legislation unconstitutional, so that 5–4 decisions against FDR became majority decisions allowing his schemes.

Wickard v. Filburn, the most fanciful of these decisions, as we've seen, absurdly ruled that the Commerce Clause gave the federal government the power to regulate the amount of grain a farmer could grow to feed to his own livestock, even though agriculture isn't commerce and the grain didn't enter into interstate commerce or indeed into any commerce at all. Still, the chastened Court ruled, the grain "substantially affected" the national economy—the first time it had invoked that criterion—and thus Washington had power over it.[4]

In his dissent in *Gonzalez v. Raich* in 2005, Thomas denied that the Commerce Clause gave Congress the power to regulate a homegrown agricultural product that never entered into any commerce whatsoever, implicitly delegitimizing *Wickard*, which he cites, and thus much of the New Deal and the fast-and-loose jurisprudence that justified it. *Raich* involved two chronically ill Californians who grew and used marijuana to control their pain, thinking themselves protected by California's legalization of medical marijuana. The Feds thought otherwise. They seized six marijuana plants and charged the invalids with violating the federal Controlled Substances Act. The Court sided with the Feds.

Over Thomas's strenuous dissent: the invalids, he thundered, "use marijuana that has never been bought or sold, that has never crossed state lines, and that has had no demonstrable effect on the national market for marijuana. If Congress can regulate this under the Commerce Clause, then it can regulate virtually anything—and the Federal

Government is no longer one of limited and enumerated powers." Not only does this case not concern commerce; it doesn't even concern economic activity. "If the majority is to be taken seriously, the Federal Government may now regulate quilting bees, clothes drives, and potluck suppers throughout the 50 States," he protested. In this same vein, he dissented from the Court's blessing of Obamacare's penalty for failure to buy health insurance in *NFIB* v. *Sebelius* in 2012, rejecting "the Government's unprecedented claim in this suit that it may regulate not only economic activity but also *inactivity* that substantially affects interstate commerce."[5]

———

THE COMMERCE CLAUSE was the New Deal's crudest weapon for subverting the founders' Constitution. But after considering how FDR & Co. had done it, Thomas came to see that the subversion was more complicated. The New Deal Congress wielded its enlarged authority not directly but through administrative agencies such as the Agricultural Adjustment Administration, the National Labor Relations Board, and the Securities and Exchange Commission. In several 2015 opinions, Thomas focused on how these agencies increasingly undermine the original Constitution even more insidiously than Congress's torturing of the Commerce Clause. These particular opinions are concurrences or dissents, not the Court's majority ruling, as is true of many of the justice's key opinions. Their importance lies in making what previously had been an academic and journalistic concern part of official Supreme Court jurisprudence and targeting previous rulings for future reversal. As his former law clerk Jeffrey Wall, later principal deputy solicitor general in the Trump administration, puts it, Thomas "is content to sow ideas that result later in changes in the law." Judge Gregory G. Katsas, a former clerk who now sits on Thomas's former D.C. Court of Appeals, agrees: "The justice has his view of writing for the ages."[6]

The Court has "overseen and sanctioned the growth of an administrative system that concentrates the power to make laws and the power to enforce them in the hands of a vast and unaccountable administrative apparatus that finds no comfortable home in our constitutional structure," Thomas lamented in his concurrence in *Department of Transportation v. Association of American Railroads*, echoing FDR's words but not his gently bemused tone. "The end result may be trains that run on time (although I doubt it), but the cost is to our Constitution and the individual liberty it protects." Since the high court remanded the complex railroad-rate-setting case back to the lower courts, he set out some principles for the guidance of those courts and the consideration of his colleagues in future cases.[7]

The combination in the same hands of the power to make the laws and the power to carry them out is the essence of arbitrary rule by decree, the founders believed, guided by such writers as the Baron de Montesquieu, John Locke, and William Blackstone. For them, the separation of powers was key to the protection of liberty from such tyranny, Thomas writes. The Constitution vested *all* legislative power in Congress, *all* executive power in the president, and *all* judicial power in the Supreme Court and inferior courts, because the framers did not want to have those powers delegated to other hands, lest it bring about the "gradual concentration of the several powers in the same department," as Madison put it in *Federalist 51*. As Locke himself had said, Thomas reminds his colleagues, "The legislative cannot transfer the power of making laws to any other hands: for it being but a delegated power from the people, they who have it cannot pass it over to others."

Sure enough, the delegation of legislative powers to the administrative agencies, whose rules bind citizens and thus are laws in all but name, results in just such a dangerous concentration, which the Court permitted by gradual and almost careless application of an "intelligible purpose" test. Originally, the test concerned the very narrow case of a tariff law that left it to the president to determine if the conditions that the law had set for changes in the rate had been met, a factual determination that, as a later decision pointed out, did not concern questions of justice or expediency—policy questions that demand a legislative determination. But, Thomas observed, the Court forgot this narrow qualification and in time allowed Congress to delegate its lawmaking power to agencies without reservation.

———

"Perhaps we deliberately departed from the separation [of powers], bowing to the exigencies of modern Government that were so often cited in cases upholding challenged delegations of rulemaking authority," Thomas muses. Perhaps, as an earlier Court conceded in a Wilsonian mood, he notes, "our jurisprudence has been driven by a practical understanding that in our increasingly complex society, replete with ever changing and more technical problems, Congress simply cannot do its job absent an ability to delegate power under broad general directives."

However practical that delegation might seem, it is unconstitutional in multiple, fundamental ways. "To understand the 'intelligible principle' test as permitting Congress to delegate policy judgment in this context is to divorce that test from its history," Thomas objects. "We should return to the original meaning of the Constitution: The Government may create generally applicable rules of private conduct only through the proper exercise of legislative power. I accept that this would inhibit the Government from acting with the speed and efficiency Congress has sometimes found desirable." But that's a virtue of constitutional lawmaking, not a flaw. As Hamilton put it in *Federalist* 73, "The injury which may possibly be done by defeating a few good laws will be amply compensated by the advantage of preventing a number of bad ones."

———

It's worth pausing to note how ingrained and reflexive such delegation has grown. During the 2017 Senate Judiciary Committee confirmation hearings of Judge Neil Gorsuch as a Supreme Court justice, there was something almost endearingly obtuse in Senator Dianne Feinstein's placid explanation that there is "a long-standing legal doctrine that allows agencies to write regulations necessary to effectively implement the laws that Congress passes and the president signs. Congress relies on agency experts to write the specific rules, regulations, guidelines, and procedures necessary to carry out laws we enact"—the rules that enable "the Clean Air Act and the Clean Water Act to protect our environment from pollution," and allow "the FDA and the agriculture department [to] safeguard the health and safety of our food supply, our water, our medicines."

"We in Congress rely on the scientists, biologists, economists, engineers, and other experts to help ensure our laws are effectively implemented," the senator went on, now waxing lyrical. "For example, even though Dodd-Frank was passed nearly seven years ago to combat the rampant abuse that led to our country's worst financial crisis since the Great Depression, it still requires over a hundred regulations to be implemented by the Securities and Exchange Commission, the Commodity Futures Trading Commission, and other regulators in order to reach its full effectiveness, as intended by Congress when it was passed."

The senator's naivety grew increasingly horrifying the longer her complacent description of these infinitely multiplying agencies and regulations, like something out of "The Sorcerer's Apprentice," went on. What she was saying is that the American people no longer govern themselves by laws that they themselves have made through their senators and congressmen. Legislators instead gauge some vague national feeling, articulate it by decreeing, "Let there be clean air and water," and set loose an army of supposed experts to make a maze of rules ensuring that their broad and general vision becomes reality, in whatever form and by whatever means the experts deem best. This process, the senator admitted—or, rather, boasted—"has been fundamental to how our government addresses real world challenges in our country and has been in place for decades." True, but it's not democracy.[8]

Moreover, history shows that the joke is on the senator as well as on the people. The "experts" charged with effecting the legislators' orders have in practice perverted those directives, making them mean precisely the opposite of what the law plainly states. We saw in the last chapter how two Department of Health, Education, and Welfare directives almost instantly transformed the 1964 Civil Rights Act's prohibition against discriminating by race in school assignment into a demand to discriminate on just that basis. Similarly, a 1970 edict from Labor Department bureaucrats, backed up by HEW's Civil Rights Office, decreed that Titles VI and VII of the Civil Rights Act, concerning hiring in public institutions and even in private colleges that accept federal grants, must satisfy race and sex quotas. As with school assignment quotas, the courts were all too willing to endorse this perversion of the law, so that by 1980 a federal judge felt empowered to order the New York Police Department to make sure its qualifying exam for recruits produced the "right" number of minorities and women. Even entirely private all-male clubs had to admit women under the judicial overseer's lash.[9] If there is such a thing as a right to privacy, it is here: government has no business invading and regulating the self-governing institutions of civil society.

IF THE DELEGATION of legislative power to executive agencies is illegitimate, the delegation of judicial power is a special affront to judges like Thomas. That power was never Congress's to begin with, so how can it delegate what Article III of the Constitution doesn't give it? Yet bizarrely, the Supreme Court itself, in a World War II price-control case, *Bowles v. Seminole Rock & Sand*, "requires judges to defer to agency interpretations of regulations,…giving legal effect to the interpretations rather than the regulations themselves," Thomas complained in *Perez v. Mortgage Bankers Association* in 2015. That doctrine of deference, Thomas objects, has now taken on a life of its own, so that judges defer to agency interpretations not only of their own regulations but of other agencies' regulations and even of criminal sentencing—and even when an interpretation differs from a previous interpretation of the same regulation, so that it amounts to new, flamboyantly illegitimate lawmaking that is utterly confusing to the citizens the regulation binds.

You can never be sure—especially if you are a businessman—if you are breaking "the law" or not.[10]

For the framers, separation of powers wasn't protection enough against tyranny. They also designed a system of checks and balances to prevent an improper accumulation of power in any one branch. The judiciary plays a critical role in this dynamic equipoise, and failure to exercise its independent judgment of what is lawful for executive-branch agency actions amounts to a gross dereliction of duty, Thomas charges. After all, the framers carefully protected judicial independence with lifetime tenure and irreducible salaries, insulations against the pressure of public opinion that they purposely withheld from the other two branches, subject to the discipline of regular elections. "You don't review cases when you say, 'Oh, we defer to virtually everything the agency does,'" Thomas said in 2016. "We don't do that to district judges, and district judges are Article III judges."[11] The Supreme Court should give agency interpretations a tighter, not a looser, scrutiny than it gives district or appeals court decisions—especially since agency bureaucrats have tenure almost as secure and unaccountable as judges have.

"Probably the most oft-recited justification for *Seminole Rock* deference is that of agency expertise in administering technical statutory schemes," Thomas writes in *Perez*. But that defense "misidentifies the relevant inquiry. The proper question faced by courts in interpreting a regulation is not what the best policy choice might be, but what the regulation means." And who better than a judge to analyze the meaning of the language of a law or regulation?

Finally, in *Michigan* v. *EPA*, Thomas concluded that what goes for *Seminole Rock* deference goes equally for the deference doctrine pronounced in *Chevron* v. *Natural Resources Defense Council* in 1984. That *Chevron* doctrine assumes "that Congress, when it left ambiguity in a statute meant for implementation by an agency, understood that the ambiguity would be resolved, first and foremost, by the agency, and desired the agency (rather than the courts) to possess whatever degree of discretion the ambiguity allows." Nevertheless, when an agency interprets a regulation, Thomas writes, its sub-rosa lawmaking cries out for judicial review. Deference, in other words, improperly forces judges "to abandon what they believe is 'the best reading of an ambiguous statute' in favor of an agency's construction. It thus wrests from Courts the ultimate interpretative authority to 'say what the law is'"—precisely the authority that Chief Justice John Marshall claimed for the judiciary in *Marbury v. Madison*. That can hardly be constitutional.[12] In this vein it's not surprising that the Trump administration's lion-hearted scourge of administrative-state regulations, Neomi Rao, head of the Office of Information and Regulatory Affairs, is a former Thomas clerk, as are a significant number of key administration officials and federal judges, including 20 percent of the appellate judges President Trump has appointed.[13]

———

THOMAS'S MAGNUM OPUS so far, *McDonald v. Chicago*, is a textbook demonstration of his method of judging. Here, with his characteristic skepticism toward *stare decisis*, he utterly repudiates the Supreme Court's most tragically wrong and history-changing decisions of them all, the *Slaughter-House Cases* and *United States v. Cruikshank*, the two cases (examined in the preceding chapter) that strangled Reconstruction in its cradle and licensed the generations-long grip of Jim Crow on black Southerners. He shows that the Court in those cases bloody-mindedly misinterpreted both how the framers of the Fourteenth Amendment understood the language in which they couched it and how contemporary commentators heard that language. He demonstrates that that original understanding belongs to an unbroken intellectual tradition deriving from Magna Carta and the English Bill of Rights. It was asserted in the American colonies at least as early as 1636, was affirmed in the Declaration of Independence, and was powerfully restated by Lincoln as an anti-slavery rationale. And vibrating throughout Thomas's 2010 *McDonald* concurrence is a note of pained indignation that his own Court in earlier days could have participated in overturning the equality of rights that so many had given their lives to uphold—an equality that at long last it should reassert explicitly.[14]

So, to describe his fully mature method of constitutional interpretation more precisely: he begins with the plain command of the constitutional text or amendment in question, locates it in all the concrete complexity of its historical context, traces the historical process by which the command got distorted from its original meaning, explains the real-world consequences of that distortion, and points out how the Court can repair the damage going forward. His goal is a return to the framers' vision, aimed at protecting the liberty he cherishes as dearly as they did.

The American founders well knew, Thomas writes in *McDonald*, that slavery was "irreconcilable with the principles of equality, government by consent, and inalienable rights proclaimed by the Declaration of Independence and embedded in our constitutional structure," but they couldn't end the evil institution, which their generation inherited rather than created, if they wanted to get the Constitution ratified. Seven decades later, the nation fought a bloody Civil War to resolve that contradiction, on "the leading principle—the sheet anchor of American republicanism," in Lincoln's phrase, that "no man is good enough to govern another man, *without that other's consent.*" After the war, the Fourteenth Amendment sought to heal the wound that slavery had left behind. The amendment began by unambiguously declaring—contrary to the Supreme Court's 1857 holding in *Dred Scott*—that black Americans were citizens of the United States and of the state wherein they resided. *Full* citizens, the amendment went on to say: for it commanded that "[n]o State shall make or enforce any law which shall abridge the privileges or immunities of citizens of the United States."

What were those privileges and immunities? The English-speaking peoples, from the time they began to discuss law, have understood that "privileges and immunities" means the basic rights of citizenship—government protection of life, liberty, and property, Thomas explains. The 1765 *Massachusetts Resolves*, for instance, equates the rights "which are founded in the Law of God and Nature, and are the common Rights of

Mankind" with the "essential Rights, Liberties, Privileges and Immunities of the people of Great Britain" and of Britain's American colonies. Treaties ceding the Louisiana and Florida territories to the United States in 1803 and 1819 reflexively assured the new inhabitants that they would be admitted, "according to the principles of the federal Constitution, to the enjoyments of all the privileges, rights, and immunities, of the citizens of the United States."

In the years just after the Civil War, the formula similarly meant the full panoply of constitutional rights, as witness President Andrew Johnson's proclamation of amnesty to Confederates, which restored "all rights, privileges, and immunities under the Constitution." The framers of the Fourteenth Amendment meant no less. Representative John Bingham, its chief draftsman, declared that the amendment would "secur[e] to all the citizens in every State all the privileges and immunities of citizens," and it would "arm the Congress of the United States, by the consent of the people . . . , with the power to enforce the bill of rights as it stands in the Constitution today." Further, said Senator Jacob Howard during the debates on the amendment, its aim was prohibiting the states "from abridging the privileges and immunities of the citizens of the United States," including "the personal rights guaranteed and secured by the first eight amendments of the Constitution." That was how contemporaries understood the amendment: a typical commentator wrote in 1868 that the rights guaranteed by Article IV of the Constitution and the Bill of Rights, "which had been construed to apply only to the national government, are thus imposed upon the States."

———

THE REASON that there is any question about whether the Fourteenth Amendment applies the Bill of Rights to the states is that, in the aftermath of the Civil War, Southern whites did not want blacks to arm themselves. And they prevailed. So while it's true that the Court's precedents deny that the Fourteenth Amendment bans states from abridging the rights that the first eight amendments protect, including the right to bear arms at issue in *McDonald v. Chicago*, those precedents are as unsavory as they are incoherent, and they should have been overruled long ago, Thomas argues.

Only eight years after the Confederacy's defeat and five years after the Fourteenth Amendment's ratification, he notes, *Slaughter-House* ruled that the rights protected by the federal and state governments were not identical and that the Fourteenth Amendment protected only federal rights, which were limited to such matters as using the nation's seaports and enjoying its protection on the high seas, and perhaps the right of peaceful assembly and *habeas corpus* (as chapter 3 recounted). The Bill of Rights? Not really. Going further, the Court's shameful 1876 *Cruikshank* ruling that set free perpetrators of the 1873 Colfax Massacre—which historian Eric Foner calls "the bloodiest single instance of racial carnage in the Reconstruction era"—"is not a precedent entitled to any respect," Thomas acerbically and unarguably concludes, the more so because of its consequences. Without federal enforcement of the freedmen's inalienable right to keep and bear arms, the armed thugs of the Ku Klux Klan and their ilk could "subjugate the newly freed slaves and their descendants through a wave of private violence designed to drive blacks from the voting booth and force them into peonage, an effective return to slavery."

Typical was (later governor and U.S. senator) Pitchfork Ben Tillman's cold-blooded massacre in South Carolina of "a troop of black militiamen for no other reason than that they had dared to conduct a celebratory Fourth of July parade through their mostly black town," Thomas writes. Imagine: they celebrated the Declaration of Independence! But for decades, groups like Tillman's "raped, murdered, lynched, and robbed as a means of intimidating, and instilling pervasive fear in, those whom they despised....Between 1882 and 1968, there were at least 3,446 reported lynching of blacks in the South."

Only firearms could protect those blacks, and only sometimes. Still, Thomas writes, "One young man recalled the night during his childhood when his father stood armed at a jail until morning to ward off lynchers. The experience left him with a sense, 'not of powerless-

ness, but of the possibilities of salvation' that came from standing up
to intimidation." Thomas's grandfather, who worked so hard to instill
the old American virtues of self-reliance and personal responsibility in
him, would heartily approve.

———

THOMAS'S FELLOW JUSTICES in *McDonald*, with reverence for *stare decisis*—meaning in this case for *Slaughter-House* and *Cruikshank*—had
employed a long-standing judicial workaround of the privileges or
immunities issue. The right to keep arms is fundamental to our nation's
particular scheme of ordered liberty and system of justice, the Court
ruled, and therefore, through the venerable doctrine of "substantive due
process," which holds that the Fourteenth Amendment's due process
clause goes beyond procedural safeguards and makes some rights so
basic that no state can withdraw them, both the Second and Fourteenth
Amendments prohibit Chicago from banning residents from keeping
handguns in their homes.

For his part, Thomas always cares that the Court not only should
reach the right conclusion but should get there through correct legal
reasoning, faithful to the original text. He makes short work of the
"substantive due process" notion. It is smoke and mirrors, more fictional
than most legal fictions. "Moreover, this fiction is a particularly dangerous one," Thomas writes, since the Court has found no authoritative
basis for distinguishing "'fundamental' rights that warrant protection
from nonfundamental rights that do not," allowing judges excessive
"flexibility" in interpretation, which has led them to invent, rather than
to interpret, law. Indeed, a mountain of erroneous judgments rests on
this doctrine, so while junking it would play extensive havoc with *stare
decisis*, that's an infinitely better path than piling error upon error by
continuing a hokey dodge around an old but incorrect, blood-soaked,
and disreputable reading of the Fourteenth Amendment.

Legal scholars have spilled oceans of ink considering how to balance a correct originalist interpretation against a flawed one invested

with the authority of *stare decisis*, given the weighty "reliance interests" of citizens and businesses in trusting that they are obeying what they believe is the settled rule of law. Wouldn't a jolt to *stare decisis* spark chaos and instability?

One answer has been that the Court doesn't hesitate to overturn statutes, the enactments of the people's elected representatives, when it thinks them mistakenly unconstitutional. Even so, order prevails. So why should the justices hesitate to overturn the opinions of their unelected judicial predecessors when they believe them in error? Though Thomas himself never systematically addresses the intricacies of how the Court and Congress can ensure order after the overturning of a major precedent—hardly an impossible prudential task—he is clear in the present case that maintaining the existing fiction not only is subversive of governmental legitimacy but also has led and will lead to further distortions of the Constitution, and it has permitted a monumental historical lie to fester instead of allowing the clear sunlight of truth to disinfect and heal it. In his view, it's infinitely better—in this case and in future ones—to put aside substantive due process and *stare decisis*, to overrule *Slaughter-House* and *Cruikshank*, and straightforwardly to apply the Fourteenth Amendment's privileges or immunities clause as its framers meant it to be understood.

———

JUAN WILLIAMS declared in 2015 that "Clarence Thomas is now leading the national debate on race," and three Thomas opinions, which together form a single argument—*Adarand v. Peña, Missouri v. Jenkins,* and *Grutter v. Bollinger*—bear out that large claim.[15] In his concurrence in *Adarand*, a 1995 case testing the lawfulness of bonuses to government subcontractors who employ blacks or Hispanics, Thomas held that there's no moral or constitutional difference "between laws designed to subjugate a race and those that distribute benefits on the basis of race in order to foster some current notion of equality. Government cannot make us equal; it can only recognize, respect, and protect us as equal before the law." Discrimination, whether ill or well intentioned, subverts the core American principle that all men are created equal. Insidiously, "positive" discrimination "teaches many that because of chronic and apparently immutable handicaps, minorities cannot compete with them without their patronizing indulgence." How can such discrimination fail to prompt hurtful feelings of superiority or resentment in the majority and dependence and a sense of entitlement among minorities?[16]

That same year, Thomas's take-no-prisoners concurrence in *Missouri v. Jenkins*—a case ending federal district judge Russell Clark's years-long, Ahab-like quest to impose his megalomaniacal version of racial justice on the Kansas City, Missouri, schools—skewered seven pernicious errors in 40 years of federal race jurisprudence. First, Thomas noted that racial isolation may result not from intentional state-sponsored segregation but from "voluntary housing choices or other private decisions," which don't concern the courts. Racial imbalances are not, in themselves, unconstitutional. Second, even if you make the hard-to-prove assumption that racial imbalance is a "vestige" of past state segregation, what remedy can the courts provide to behavior that stopped 30 years ago? Third, and particularly nasty, is the assumption "that anything that is predominantly black must be inferior" and its corollary, that "segregation injures blacks because blacks, when left on their own, cannot achieve." Such racist stereotypes have no place in American courts.[17]

Fourth, the *Brown v. Board* school desegregation decision introduced into race jurisprudence a confusion that unfortunately snared Judge Clark. *Brown*, Thomas writes, "did not need to rely upon any psychological or social science research in order to announce the simple, yet fundamental truth that the Government cannot discriminate among its citizens on the basis of race." However, as Thomas is too polite to say here, it did. It accepted a tissue of social-scientific hocus-pocus involving "experiments" with black and white dolls, purporting to prove that segregation generates feelings of inferiority in black students that impairs their ability to learn. But that's neither here nor there, Thomas contends. "Segregation was not unconstitutional because it might have caused psychological feelings of inferiority," he writes, but "because the State classified students based on their race."

He spoke more plainly in a 1987 article: "*Brown* was a missed opportunity, as [are] all its progeny, whether they involve busing, affirmative action, or redistricting," he declared. The Court should have focused on reason, justice, and freedom, not sentiment, sensitivity, and dependence. A Court that wanted to "validate the *Brown* decision" would replace Chief Justice Earl Warren's decision with one more in keeping with the Constitution and the Declaration of Independence. Thomas's candidate would be Justice John Marshall Harlan's ringing 1896 dissent in *Plessy v. Ferguson* (a case that the *Brown* Court, respecting *stare decisis*, failed to overrule, except in the special case of education): "Our Constitution is color-blind and neither knows nor tolerates classes among citizens.... The law regards man as man and takes no account of his surroundings or of his color when his civil rights as guaranteed by the supreme law of the land are involved."[18]

Fifth, even compared with busing or affirmative action, Judge Clark's remedy—a megaproject of social engineering aimed at transforming the Kansas City schools into magnet schools by outfitting them with Olympic-size swimming pools, broadcast studios, model U.N. chambers wired for simultaneous translation, planetariums, even a 25-acre farm—dizzyingly exceeded the judiciary's constitutional powers to interpret the law. It was a bad enough assault upon federalism for Judge Clark to order the Kansas City school district to pay a quarter of the cost of all this. But for a federal judge to order the district to raise property taxes to pony up, and to enjoin the state from interfering: that flings down federalism and dances upon it—and, not incidentally, amounts to taxation without representation. Sixth, as this case shows, the founders were right to view with cold-eyed suspicion equity courts, with their power to impose "equitable remedies." As Thomas Jefferson put it, "Relieve the judges from the rigour of text law, and permit them, with pretorian discretion, to wander into it's equity, and the whole legal system becomes incertain."[19]

Seventh, even if Judge Clark were right that past segregation "caused a system wide reduction in student achievement," and even if his pharaonic program produced benefits—though in fact it didn't boost student performance—it would produce them for individuals who were not victims of discrimination. "A school district cannot be discriminated against on the basis of its race, because a school district has no race," Thomas observes. "It goes without saying that only individuals can suffer from discrimination, and only individuals can receive the remedy."

———

A NOTE of icy scorn runs through Thomas's opinion in *Grutter v. Bollinger*, a 2003 case in which the Court upheld affirmative-action admissions to the University of Michigan Law School. In concurring that racial preferences should end in 25 years, and dissenting to every other part of the majority's ruling, Thomas is striving for jocularity, but he seems to have run out of patience with the self-cherishing antics of overpaid bureaucrats like university president Lee Bollinger (later the longtime president of Columbia) and his fellow administrators, glowing with the virtue of their good intentions and careless of the havoc they wreak. Here they have an institution financed by the taxpayers of their state, though only 27 percent of admitted students are Michiganders and only 16 percent of graduates stay in the state. So for starters, there's no compelling state interest in having this school exist.

And there's less compelling state interest for it to admit ill-prepared minority students in order to achieve "diversity," which offers no educational benefit to anyone, despite the law school's claim. It is merely an aesthetic preference of Bollinger et al., who like a smattering of black and brown faces in their lecture halls. Too bad that the Court's majority fell for "a faddish slogan of the cognoscenti," though at least it tacked on a 25-year sunset clause to its approval of the law school's brand of affirmative action (a stipulation that confesses that *Grutter* is an exercise in social engineering, not jurisprudence). Despite precedents holding "that racial classifications are per se harmful and that almost no amount of benefit in the eye of the beholder can justify such classifications," the majority decision still clings to "the benighted notions that one can tell when racial discrimination benefits (rather than hurts) minority groups, and that racial discrimination is necessary to remedy general societal ills."

Much has been said about the supposed (but illusory) educational benefits to white students of a racially diverse class, and we know its benefits to the administration's self-regard, but what about affirmative action's supposed minority beneficiaries? "The Law School tantalizes unprepared students with the promise of a University of Michigan degree and all of the opportunities that it offers," Thomas writes. "These overmatched students take the bait, only to find that they cannot succeed in the cauldron of competition." And what about the "handful of blacks who would be admitted in the absence of racial discrimination"—like Thomas at Yale Law? "The majority of blacks are admitted to the Law School because of discrimination, and because of this policy all are tarred as undeserving." Moreover, the taint follows the deserving no matter how high they ascend and how much they achieve, Thomas says, as he well knows.

Instead of their constant "social experiments on other people's children," Thomas writes, why don't the nation's elites honor the heartfelt and prophetic plea of Frederick Douglass a century and a half ago? "What I ask for the negro is not benevolence, not pity, not sympathy, but simply justice. The American people have always been anxious to know what they shall do with us.... Do nothing with us! Your doing with us has already played the mischief with us," Douglass implores in the passage with which Thomas opens his *Grutter* opinion. "[I]f the negro cannot stand on his own legs, let him fall also. All I ask is, give him a chance to stand on his own legs!" That's one heroically self-reliant man quoting another such, whose portrait hangs behind Thomas's desk, facing copies of the Emancipation Proclamation and General William Tecumseh Sherman's Field Order No. 15, confiscating 400,000 Southern coastal acres for ownership by newly freed blacks, including Thomas's ancestors, in

40-acre plots, including a plow-mule. The country would do well to heed such hard-won advice. We fought a Civil War; we had a civil rights movement: now black Americans—and only black Americans—can work their own liberation, after half a century of social engineering that harmed both the country and its black citizens.[20]

———

PERHAPS IT's because Thomas was already pondering the ideas central to two of his key opinions in a 1994 article for *City Journal*, the magazine I then edited, that they strike me as no less profound than *McDonald v. Chicago*. In any event, his 1999 dissent in *Chicago v. Morales* and his 2007 concurrence in *Morse v. Frederick*, taken together, add up to a comprehensive account of how the Court sabotaged the order-keeping authority of two essential public institutions, the police and the public schools. What is so striking about those opinions, sweeping in their historical account of how these organizations once operated and how the Court damaged them, is Thomas's clear-eyed understanding of the consequences for the actual lives of ordinary people, especially those in inner cities. There's nothing fanciful here.

"What are the real-world effects of the 'rights revolution'—the legal revolution of the past thirty or so years [now 50-plus] in creating and expanding individual rights?" Thomas asked in *City Journal*. How did the social order and individual lives change because of judicial orders not to expel weapons-toting or disruptive kids from school or to evict drug dealers from public housing without court-supervised hearings, costly in time and money, and not to arrest vagrants or even order them to move on? The judges' tragically mistaken rationale: most unruly housing-project tenants, disorderly school kids, vagrants, panhandlers, and loitering gangbangers are poor minorities, supposed victims of society's pervasive racism and systematic denial of opportunity. Because their wildness or criminality are the natural results of these malign, external forces, punishing such behavior, for which individuals are ultimately not responsible, would be to victimize the victims even more harshly, piling injustice upon injustice. In addition, the question-authority culture of the 1960s, which placed greater value on "the excesses of self-indulgence" than on "the community's sense of decency or decorum," shaped the thinking of lawyers and judges along with everyone else and further fueled the rights revolution's unwillingness to hold individuals personally responsible for the destructive consequences of their behavior.

But, Thomas asks, if we don't punish wrongdoers, doesn't our lack of outrage tell right-doing students that we make no moral distinction between their laudable behavior and its opposite, a most destructive message? And doesn't our victimology implicitly dismiss minorities and the poor as less than fully human, when of course they are "human beings—capable of dignity as well as shame, folly as well as success. We should be treated as such." Finally, "Would the lawyers and judges making these rules want to live under the conditions that so many in the inner cities must endure," thanks to their decrees?[21]

The *Morales* dissent pulls no punches in describing those conditions, which Chicago won't be able to improve now that the Court has struck down a democratically enacted city ordinance imposing small fines or short jail terms on criminal street-gang members loitering in public places, if they don't obey a cop's order to move on. The justices considered the ordinance's restriction of personal liberties to be vague and arbitrary, and therefore unconstitutional. But they didn't seem to grasp the concrete reality of Chicago's 132 gangs, menacingly hanging out on street corners. Each year between 1987 and 1994, the city's gangbangers had committed more than 100 murders and more than 3,000 other violent crimes, terrorizing the law-abiding residents of ghetto neighborhoods and making them "prisoners in their own homes," Thomas writes—so much so that the city hired dozens of escorts for kids who otherwise would be too scared to go to school.

The Chicago City Council, in extensive hearings before it passed the ordinance, listened as inner-city residents described their terror of the streets. "I have had guns pulled on me. I have been threatened. I get intimidated on a daily basis," one woman testified. Now she asks herself,

"Do I go out today? Do I put my ax in my briefcase? Do I [dress] like a bum so I am not looking rich?" Thomas could tell his own stories, having grown up on a Savannah ghetto block that was "an island of safety tucked in between two much rougher blocks"—one of them so violent that his grandfather dubbed it the Blood Bucket and forbade his grandsons to venture there. So who counts more, the so-called victims or their law-abiding neighbors? And why are lawbreakers more truly victims than the neighbors they prey on?

———

AMERICAN COURTS, from colonial times until the Warren Court, never imagined the through-the-looking-glass world that *Morales* inhabits, so careless of public order. They saw policemen not simply as "enforcers of the criminal law," Thomas writes. Officers "have long been vested with the responsibility for preserving the public peace." That was certainly true when Congress framed the Fourteenth Amendment, which the Court majority in *Morales* also invokes on "substantive due process" grounds to justify its rejection of Chicago's ordinance. One manual for lawmen of that era directs "peace officers"—the very term is telling—"to suppress every unlawful assembly, affray, or riot which may happen in their presence," for instance. Similarly, the 1887 *New York Police Manual* orders cops to "preserve the public peace, prevent crime, detect and arrest offenders, suppress riots, mobs and insurrections, disperse unlawful or dangerous assemblages, and assemblages which obstruct the free passage of public streets, sidewalks, parks, and places."

In other words, though Thomas doesn't use the term, Americans have long taken for granted what we now call Broken Windows policing—the theory that cops can prevent crime by suppressing minor offenses against public order, thereby making clear to the unruly that the authorities are on the watch and will catch them if they commit more serious crimes, a powerful deterrent. Thomas's *Morales* dissent notes how crisply a 1904 treatise on government's police power puts it: "The criminal law deals with offenses after they have been committed, the police power aims to prevent them. The activity of the police for the prevention of crime is partly such as needs no special legal authority." Without such order-maintaining crime prevention, for which cops must be allowed some commonsense discretion, urban life becomes anarchy—as actually happened as the U.S. crime rate rocketed skyward from the late 1960s into the 1990s.

The *Morales* Court rests its decision in part on an outstandingly zany judgment written by veterans of the Warren Court, one of many from an orgy of whimsical decision-making that began in the 1960s and lasted for decades. This was the infamous *Papachristou v. City of Jacksonville*, which hamstrung order-maintenance policing ever after and helped fuel the ensuing crime explosion. Police in Jacksonville, Florida, had arrested nine people, some of them known thieves and drug dealers, for vagrancy and disorderly loitering, relying on a municipal ordinance that echoed the resonant language of Elizabethan England's vagrancy law. Justice William O. Douglas's 1972 opinion for the Court struck down the ordinance, and the state law that authorized it, for their vagueness. It's true, he conceded in *Papachristou*, that the Constitution mentions no right to loiter, but loitering, nightwalking, and other such activities that the ordinance criminalizes are "unwritten amenities [that] have been, in part, responsible for giving our people the feeling of independence and self-confidence, the feeling of creativity. These amenities have dignified the right of dissent, and have honored the right to be nonconformists and the right to defy submissiveness. They have encouraged lives of high spirits, rather than hushed, suffocating silence." And then Douglas went through the stratosphere into orbit, creating a new set of framers. "They are embedded in Walt Whitman's writings, especially in his 'Song of the Open Road.' They are reflected, too, in the spirit of Vachel Lindsay's 'I Want to Go Wandering,' and by Henry D. Thoreau." So much for four centuries of Anglo-American Broken Windows policing.[22]

Thomas, summing up his *Morales* dissent, notes that *Papachristou*, whose right-to-loiter authority Justice John Paul Stevens invokes in his *Morales* ruling for the Court, is a highly dubious precedent (which, by implication, ought to be discarded as mere "judge-made constitutional law"). The Court, by building on such a flimsy foundation and "focus[ing] extensively on the 'rights' of gang members and their companions," Thomas opines, "has denied our most vulnerable citizens the very thing that Justice Stevens elevates above all else—the 'freedom of movement.' And that is a shame."[23]

———

WHEN THOMAS criticized in *City Journal* the rights revolution's new barriers to expelling disruptive or violent kids from school, he had in mind such late-1960s cases as *In re Gault*, which ordered the juvenile courts to give delinquent kids facing reform school many of the procedural rights of adult criminal trials—a ruling that gave activist lawyers the idea that such new rights could be extended to kids facing school discipline, as well.[24] The pivotal first result of that idea was *Tinker v. Des Moines*, in which the Court ruled in 1969 that a school's punishment of the Tinker children for wearing black armbands to protest the Vietnam War had violated their First Amendment free speech rights. Unless a school can show that it forbade its pupils' free expression because it "materially and substantially interfere[d]" with school discipline, rather than because of "a mere desire to avoid the discomfort and unpleasantness that always accompany an unpopular viewpoint," the kids are free to speak their minds.[25]

This ruling, which "has undermined the traditional authority of teachers to maintain order in public schools," has no mooring whatever in the Constitution and is immaculately ignorant of the history of U.S. public education, Thomas contends in his 2007 concurrence in *Morse v. Frederick*, which he wrote to say that he would have gone further than the Court's majority and overruled *Tinker* altogether. From the first scattered appearance of U.S. public schools in the early nineteenth century up until the Court intervened in 1969, students had no free speech right. "[T]eachers taught, and students listened. Teachers commanded, and students obeyed," Thomas observes. "Rules of etiquette were enforced, and courteous behavior was demanded," just as in his grandfather's house.

No one thought the teacher's authority inappropriate. The law and the community saw him or her *in loco parentis*, that is, standing in the place of a parent. As a North Carolina court explained in 1837, Thomas notes, "One of the most sacred duties of parents, is to train up and qualify their children, for becoming useful and virtuous members of society; this duty cannot be effectually performed without the ability to command obedience, to control stubbornness, to quicken diligence, and to reform bad habits. The teacher is the substitute of the parent; . . . and in the exercise of these delegated duties, is invested with his power."

No more—though *Tinker's* absolutism proved unworkable, and the Court had to modify it in 1986, when a student delivered a speech containing "an elaborate, graphic, and explicit sexual metaphor," which the justices ruled had no place in a high school assembly. A further modification occurred in 1988. And now, in the present *Morse v. Frederick* case, ruling that a school may prohibit speech advocating illegal drug use, the Court modifies *Tinker* further, with the result, says Thomas, "that our jurisprudence now says that students have a right to speak in schools except when they don't." It would be far better, he concludes, "to dispense with *Tinker* altogether, and given the opportunity, I would do so."[26]

Especially since the pupil-rights revolution didn't stop with *Tinker*. That case led to *Goss v. Lopez*, which ruled that students suspended for spiking the punch at a high school dance couldn't be deprived of their Fourteenth Amendment entitlement without a due process hearing; and *Wood v. Strickland*, which gave kids the right—under an 1871 Ku Klux Klan act, of all things—to sue their teachers and principals for damages. In the end, school discipline crumbled, and defiance, disrespect, and disorder reigned in its stead—so that school authorities no longer remember their responsibility to acculturate students into traditional social values and couldn't do it if they wanted to.[27] As for inner-city kids, if they have to walk through streets terrifying with the threat of gang violence to reach schools where disorder rages, how will they learn the skills needed to make a living and be citizens?

———

FACED WITH the harsh reality of inner-city public schools that fail to give their students an education good enough to help them escape poverty or meaningfully "exercise the civic, political, and personal freedoms conferred by the Fourteenth Amendment," Thomas can't see why anyone would want to deny those kids a chance to try something better. But that's what a group of Ohio taxpayers had in mind when they sued to block a Cleveland school voucher program that would let those students attend private, predominantly Catholic, schools. The taxpayers claimed that such a program would violate the First Amendment's ban against the establishment of religion, as applied to the states by the Fourteenth Amendment.

Atypically, Thomas's concurrence in this 2002 case, *Zelman v. Simmons-Harris*, reads like a *cri de coeur*, focused as much on the policy outcome as on the constitutional reasoning. Whether the Fourteenth Amendment really does incorporate the First Amendment's Establishment Clause against the states is uncertain, he writes. But surely it can't be construed to invalidate a neutral school-choice program whose primary purpose is secular, not religious. "There would be a tragic irony in converting the Fourteenth Amendment's guarantee of individual liberty into a prohibition on the exercise of educational choice." Endorsing the Court majority's rejection of the taxpayers' claim, he ends with some asperity toward the "cognoscenti who oppose vouchers," though the chief villains here are the teachers' unions, not the elites who cooked up school busing and college affirmative action. "If society cannot end racial discrimination," he writes, "at least it can arm minorities with the education to defend themselves from some of discrimination's effects."[28] Apparently his college-days prayer for his heart to be purged of anger after the Harvard Square riot was only partially answered.

THE ARTISTRY with which Thomas eviscerates a judge-made protection not of the merely disorderly but of hard-core criminals in his 2018 *Carpenter v. United States* dissent is a virtuoso, Sherlockian unmasking of how judicial error upon error can yield a result as far removed from the Constitution as chalk from cheese. It's a wrongheaded result, moreover, that subverts law enforcement in a particularly chilling way in an age of terrorism, when the cell phone can be brother to the bomb. Convicted of participating in a string of armed robberies in Michigan and Ohio, Timothy Carpenter argued that police use of cell phone location data subpoenaed from nearby phone companies violated his Fourth Amendment protection against unreasonable searches and seizures, because the cops had failed to get a warrant, based on probable cause, to retrieve that cell-tower information. Chief Justice John Roberts, writing for a 5–4 majority, agreed.[29]

It is often said, and truly, that the time-tested principles of the Constitution are adaptable to modern developments that the framers never could have foreseen. But in the case of electronic eavesdropping and other telephonic communications, the Court has dramatically shown *how not to do it*, as Dickens would say. It's not that the justices didn't initially set out in the right direction. Chief Justice William Howard Taft, in one of the earliest such cases, properly wrote that the Fourth Amendment's protection of citizens from unreasonable searches of "their persons, houses, papers, and effects" does not shield them from the tapping of telephone lines outside their homes. No search had occurred, for the federal agents had not entered the suspected bootleggers' homes, and their conversations were neither persons, houses, papers, nor effects.[30]

Taft's commonsensical view prevailed until the 1960s, when the Court began to deem eavesdropping, even with no home intrusion, a Fourth Amendment violation. Thomas subjects to sweeping, if good-humored, ridicule the second Justice Harlan's 1967 concurrence in *Katz v. United States*, which by the 1970s had hardened into a mechanically applied "*Katz* test" for judging when Fourth Amendment protection applies. To the *Katz* Court's conclusion that a bugging device stuck outside a public phone booth overstepped the Fourth Amendment—which protects people, not places, the justices asserted, without reference to the text—Harlan added the explanation that what the amendment really protects is a person's reasonable expectation of privacy. Talk about channeling the spirit of the age! Had not Justice Douglas, only two years earlier, conjured up a right to privacy out of the Constitution's emanations and penumbras in *Griswold?* And from where did Harlan get his "reasonable expectation" test? From a brand-new law school graduate's contention in oral argument that this issue in *Katz* was "not too dissimilar from the tort 'reasonable man' test." Not too dissimilar![31]

What would the framers have to say about this? Thomas asks. For starters, they wouldn't consider the violation of someone's "reasonable expectation of privacy" a search—which is what the Fourth Amendment protects against. To them, as Thomas points out, citing dictionaries from 1770 up to Noah Webster's 1828 classic, a search meant, in Dr. Johnson's representative formulation, an "[i]nquiry by looking into every suspected place." No such thing—that is, no search, as the framers would understand it—has occurred here.

Second, the word "privacy" appears nowhere in the Constitution, not even in the Fourth Amendment. What concerned the framers of that amendment was the security of property—private property, we might call it, but property nonetheless. In particular, they remembered the much-feared colonial-era British writs of assistance—general warrants allowing customs officials to search anyplace they liked for contraband smuggled in defiance of the increasingly hated Navigation Acts. The colonists had viewed these searches as violations both of the social compact protecting liberty and property and of the ancient British principle that "every man's house is looked upon by the law to be his castle," as Blackstone had put it. Despite Harlan's contention, as even "the majority opinion in *Katz* recognized," Thomas quotes, "the Fourth Amendment 'cannot be translated into a general constitutional "right to privacy,'" as its protections 'often have nothing to do with privacy at all.'" And indeed, Thomas remarks, "Even Justice Harlan, four years after penning his concurrence in *Katz*, confessed that the test encouraged 'the substitution of words for analysis.'"

Third, in addition to reading "privacy" arbitrarily into the text, Harlan also reads out "persons, houses, papers, and effects," because, as Thomas observes, those words "cannot mean 'anywhere' or 'anything.'" To say that "'the Fourth Amendment protects people, not places,' is not a serious attempt to reconcile the constitutional text." Also read out of the text is the word "their" in the amendment's guarantee to secure people from unreasonable searches of "*their* persons, houses, papers, and effects." At the very least, Thomas writes, the word can't mean "that individuals have Fourth Amendment rights in *someone else's* property," that is, in someone else's house or premises. But that is what Harlan's opinion, and the *Katz* test that grew out of it, came to mean. In this current case, Thomas objects, the majority is taking this notion to new depths of absurdity by accepting that armed-robber Carpenter has a Fourth Amendment right of privacy in the phone companies' business records—that is, in *someone else's papers*. What law officers examined by no means belonged to Carpenter. "He did not create the records, he does not maintain them, he cannot control them, and he cannot destroy them," Thomas emphasized. "Neither the terms of his contracts nor any provision of the law makes the records his."

Finally, Thomas asks, giving the knife one more twist into the *Katz* test, what is a "reasonable" expectation of privacy? His friend Justice Scalia had already wryly answered in earlier opinions that it is whatever "this Court considers reasonable"—a policy determination, in other words, not a legal one. That's why, Scalia counseled, "[t]hough we know ourselves to be eminently reasonable, self-awareness of eminent reasonableness is not really a substitute for democratic election." And the last irony of *Carpenter*, Thomas points out, is that the people's democratically elected Congress had already crafted detailed rules for the handling of email and other stored Internet data in criminal investigations in 1986—rules it could readily adapt to cell phone data, though *Carpenter* had in effect (and probably inadvertently) invalidated them.

———

THOUGH THOMAS DENIED that schoolchildren have the right of free speech, he has otherwise been a First Amendment absolutist—based on the framers' and ratifiers' original understanding of the Constitution and the history of the particular issue, as always, and unafraid to junk precedents that don't comport with that understanding. In these cases, his underlying assumption has been that if Americans, as self-governing citizens of a democratic republic, are free to choose—in matters both political and economic—they must have all the information needed to make rational choices, so everybody must be free to impart all relevant facts and opinions.

In this line of opinions, you can watch Thomas refine his thinking as he grapples with complexities, clarifying the issue in his own mind and ultimately beginning to persuade his colleagues. In his first commercial speech case on the Court, for example, he joined Chief Justice William Rehnquist's dissent, holding that commercial speech deserves lesser First Amendment protection than political speech, since for-profit speech more easily can take care of itself than political or religious speech.[32] But writing for the Court in *Rubin v. Coors* in 1995, he began to change his view.

The federal ban on publishing a beer's alcohol content on its labels, he now wrote, is an unconstitutional infringement of free speech. The government may well be correct in saying that the ban protects the health and safety of citizens by suppressing beer "strength wars"— competition among brewers as to whose product can get you drunker faster. But in its 1980 *Central Hudson* decision, the Court had devised a test to determine the constitutionality of any government effort to regulate lawful and truthful commercial speech such as this. Does the regulation directly advance the governmental interest asserted? Is it no more extensive than necessary? The beer label ban, Thomas wrote, fails this test, because the government had not proved its claim that the ban would protect public health and minimize the social costs of alcoholism. It merely asserted that "common sense" leads to this conclusion. But in that case, why does it *require* wine and liquor labels to disclose alcohol content? Moreover, it could achieve its stated policy goal by means that don't affront the First Amendment—by directly limiting the permitted alcohol content of beer, for example.[33]

When the Court devises such judge-created multifactor balancing tests for deciding if something is constitutional, it's generally safe to guess that the justices have tried to slide around a categorical Bill of Rights command, making negotiable what is absolute, as Thomas came to see more clearly in his 1996 concurrence in another alcohol case, *44 Liquormart v. Rhode Island*. A discount liquor store, fined for breaking a state law banning the advertising of prices except in the store itself, claimed that the law violated the proprietor's First Amendment speech right. Applying the *Central Hudson* balancing test, the Court majority ruled that the state had indeed trespassed on the First Amendment, because it couldn't show that its advertising ban significantly decreases drinking.

The Court reached the correct conclusion, Thomas wrote, but its reasoning was flawed. It should have abandoned the *Central Hudson* test as illegitimate: the government has no right "to keep legal users of a product or service ignorant in order to manipulate their choices in the marketplace." It cannot "do covertly what it might not have been able to muster the political support to do openly." Far better than "this highly paternalistic approach" is the tack an earlier Court took in "assum[ing] that information is not in itself harmful, that people will perceive their own best interests, if only they are well enough informed, and that the best means to that end is to open the channels of communication rather than to close them." In fact, "'the proper allocation of resources' in our free enterprise system requires that consumer decisions be 'intelligent and well informed.'" From a First Amendment viewpoint, therefore, Thomas had come to believe, there is no "philosophical or historical basis for asserting that 'commercial' speech is of 'lower value' than 'non-commercial' speech."

More important, "democratic decisionmaking" also depends on intelligent free choices based on complete information, and once government starts "manipulating consumer choices or public opinion through the suppression of accurate 'commercial' information," there's no reason for it not to start manipulating political choices by the same means. "It is precisely this kind of choice, between the dangers of suppressing information, and the dangers of its misuse, that the First Amendment makes for us," the earlier Court had correctly observed. A true reading of the First Amendment makes clear that "all attempts to dissuade legal choices by citizens by keeping them ignorant are impermissible."[34]

———

CURIOUSLY, the toughest obstacle Thomas has faced so far in vindicating the First Amendment's guarantee of free *political* speech is the campaign finance reform movement, which presents itself as the purest of squeaky-clean advances but is nothing of the sort. In practice, laws designed to limit the amount of money spent on political campaigns turn out to be "an incumbent's protection racket," says former federal election commissioner Bradley A. Smith. Campaign contribution caps kick in just when a challenger has won name recognition roughly equal to the incumbent's, as Smith described the situation when Thomas began to address it, so that "just as a challenger starts to become competitive, campaign spending limits choke off political competition."[35]

The first such measure, the 1907 Tillman Act—named for its sponsor, Democratic senator Pitchfork Ben Tillman, whom we last encountered massacring black militiamen in his native South Carolina in July 1876 to "teach the Negroes a lesson" about daring to vote—banned corporate campaign contributions. Tillman "was concerned that the corporations, Republican corporations, were favorable toward blacks, and he felt that there was a need to regulate them," Justice Thomas noted in a 2010 speech. With such origins, Thomas remarked, it is foolhardy to assume campaign finance reform is "some sort of beatific action."[36]

The tangled campaign finance regime that Thomas set out to challenge flowed from the Tillman Act's ban on corporate (and, after

1947, union) contributions, complicated by a 1972 law and its 1974 amendment that capped individuals' political giving and spending and required public disclosure of those activities. The law also limited candidate spending, regulated contributions to and by political action committees, and set up the Federal Election Commission to police these rules, which soon covered 33 flavors of political speech and 71 kinds of speakers. The Supreme Court only worsened the confusion in its 1976 *Buckley* v. *Valeo* decision. It removed spending caps for individuals and groups, even while upholding contribution limits, and it legalized soft money for issue ads that don't explicitly call for voting for or against a given candidate.[37]

Surveying this dizzying tangle in his 2000 *Nixon* v. *Shrink Missouri* dissent, his first major campaign finance opinion, Thomas felt the need to restate some basic truths to bring some order to the confusion, now that the majority had worsened the mess by redefining the "corruption" that campaign contribution caps supposedly prevent. Let's remember, he begins, that "political speech is the primary object of First Amendment protection,... because a self-governing people depends upon the exchange of political information," especially during political campaigns. So why is the Court weakening the protection of such speech by constraining the contributions that generate it, when it has spent half a century extending First Amendment protection to such infinitely lower kinds of so-called speech as "making false defamatory statements, filing lawsuits, dancing nude, exhibiting drive-in movies with nudity, burning flags, and wearing military uniforms?"[38]

Don't the justices realize that *Buckley*'s distinction of campaign contributions from campaign spending is false? There is no difference: they are two sides of the same coin. Sure, campaign contributions generate speech by proxy, at one step removed from the giver, but the speech that campaign spending facilitates is also indirect, in that the candidate uses the money to deliver his message by broadcast or print advertising. So *Buckley*'s distinction is without a difference, and the rest of the decision's logic collapses if the direct speech versus speech-by-proxy dichotomy is false. And therefore the Court should overrule *Buckley*.

But look how the majority in this present case, *Shrink Missouri*, is making things worse. The *Buckley* Court had claimed that the government's ground for any regulation of political speech is the prevention of actual or apparent corruption, meaning the sale of political favors for contributions, in violation of the public trust—in other words, bribery—which is already illegal and needs no further measures to make it more so. But the real or apparent corruption that *Shrink Missouri* imagines is something more ineffable, something like the dictionary definition: "the perversion of anything from an original state of purity." But what might that mean as applied to politics? It can't mean "that politicians should be free from attachments to constituent groups." That is what representative democracy *is*.

So what might be the harm from which the *Shrink Missouri* majority aims to protect us? The majority, Thomas writes, "does not explicitly rely on the 'harm' that the Court in *Buckley* rejected out of hand, namely, that speech could be regulated to equalize the voices of citizens." And so the justices fall back on "vague and unenumerated harms to suffice as a compelling reason for the government to smother political speech."

———

BUT AS THOMAS makes clear in his next big campaign finance opinion, his partial concurrence and partial dissent in *McConnell v. FEC* in 2003, he thinks the harm that the *Shrink Missouri* Court was afraid to name explicitly is precisely the "harm" against which the Court's stream of campaign finance rulings implicitly—and illegitimately—protects. *McConnell* was the case that declared constitutional the next clampdown on campaign finance, the 2002 McCain-Feingold Act, which barred political parties from taking soft money and blocked union and corporate political ad spending shortly before an election. At the time, it was hard not to think that the law grew, at least in part, out of an embarrassed Senator John McCain's wish to transfer the blame to "the system" for his having unwittingly helped a constituent and contributor who turned out to be a $3 billion savings-and-loan fraudster.

If *Shrink Missouri* ratified a "sweeping repression of political speech," *McConnell*, by limiting spending as well as contributions, upholds "the most significant abridgment of the freedoms of speech and association since the Civil War," in Thomas's outraged view. It does so by relying on a 1990 decision, *Austin v. Michigan Chamber of Commerce*, that claimed to safeguard against a different kind of campaign finance corruption than the usual financial quid pro quo. *Austin* purported to save citizens from the "corrosive and distorting effects of immense aggregations of wealth that are accumulated with the help of the corporate form and that have little or no correlation to the public's support for the corporation's political ideas." These "corrosive and distorting effects," Thomas points out, "are that corporations, on behalf of their shareholders, will be able to convince voters of the correctness of their ideas." What is this but the idea that *Buckley* rejected, that the government should equalize the voices of voters, so that money should not talk in political campaigns?

Here it's worth stepping back from Thomas and the Court to survey all this from the perspective of the framers, particularly that of Constitution architect James Madison and his argument in favor of adopting the new governmental framework in *Federalist* 10. We have designed a government that will protect our natural rights to life, liberty, and property, Madison says. But since men, though equal in rights, have different talents and ambitions, the Constitution's protection of their freedom to employ those talents as they see fit will result in quite different—that is, unequal—outcomes. Some will be rich; some poor. That is not a flaw but a sign that the liberty we value is alive and well.

The great danger in a democratic republic, Madison thought, was the ganging together of the many to trample the rights of the few. As a practical matter, this tyranny of the majority, as he called it, would take the form of the unpropertied many expropriating the property of the rich, by unfair taxation, by the abolition of debt, by inflation, or by the call for communal ownership—all of which occurred during the Revolutionary War. The constitutional machinery of limited and enumerated powers, separation of powers, and checks and balances all aimed to prevent such an "improper or wicked project," and America's vast size, even in 1787, ensured that a multitude of factions—special interests—would bar any single one from tyrannizing over the others. Even so, Madison envisioned a Senate of the wise and propertied as a ballast to the more democratic branches of government, and he was troubled when the Great Compromise of the Constitutional Convention, giving two senators to each state, sank that scheme. So the idea that property should not be able to speak energetically to protect itself would be contrary to the Constitution's animating spirit.

In this sense, Thomas is accurately channeling Madison when he says, "I would overturn *Austin* and hold that the potential for corporations and unions to influence voters, via independent expenditures aimed at convincing these voters to adopt particular views, is not a form of corruption justifying any state regulation or suppression." And the implicit assumption underlying *Shrink Missouri*, *Austin*, and *McConnell*—the assumption that the state can and should equalize all voices—is only another one of those improper or wicked projects that governments, even democratic ones, periodically undertake.[39]

———

THOMAS'S MCCONNELL OPINION proved prophetic in more ways than one. Seven years later, in the celebrated 2010 *Citizens United v. FEC* case, the Court followed his advice, overturning *Austin* and allowing corporate campaign spending, partly impelled by an accurate prediction he had made in *McConnell* about where Court endorsement of McCain-Feingold's ban on such spending would lead. "The chilling endpoint of the Court's reasoning is not difficult to foresee: outright regulation of the press," he warned in *McConnell*. After all, media companies are corporations, indistinguishable from any other corporations. Their commentary influences public opinion and sways votes. "What is to stop a future Congress from determining that the press is 'too influential,' and that the 'appearance of corruption' is significant when media corporations endorse candidates or run 'slanted' or 'biased' news stories in favor of candidates or parties?" No principle enunciated in *McConnell* could stop a future Congress from enacting, and a future Court from approving, outright editorial regulation. And that means that the freedom of the press, described in the debates over constitutional ratification as "'one of the greatest bulwarks of liberty,' could be next on the chopping block."

Sure enough, in oral argument during *Citizens United*—a case overturning McCain-Feingold's ban on a conservative nonprofit corporation's release of the anti-Clinton *Hillary: The Movie* just before the 2008 primary—Justice Samuel Alito stopped the solicitor general in mid-sentence as he was defending the ban, to ask whether his argument could be applied not only to distributing the movie but also to making the same anti-Hillary case in a book. Yes, said the government's lawyer, to stunned gasps from the audience and Alito's comment that "That's pretty incredible." By the time the solicitor general was done, he had averred that the government could ban a door-stopper book containing a single anti-Hillary sentence—and the Court promptly voided that part of McCain-Feingold.[40]

THOMAS WROTE a separate opinion in *Citizens United* to point out how prophetic another major point in his *McConnell* opinion had proved. In disagreement with all of his *McConnell* colleagues, he alone had deemed McCain-Feingold's disclosure requirements unconstitutional. In that case, citing his own 1995 concurrence in *McIntyre v. Ohio Elections Commission*, he reiterated that "an author's decision to remain anonymous...is an aspect of the freedom of speech protected by the First Amendment." After all, just as you can't forbid protected speech, you also can't compel it, and disclosure requirements do just that—force citizens to attach their names to political speech or to activities that promote it.

By the time of its founding, America had already had a long, hardwon tradition of anonymous pamphleteering, as Thomas recounts with gusto in his *McIntyre* opinion. Perhaps the most famous trial of the colonial period was the 1735 *Zenger* case, in which a tyrannical New York royal governor tried to squeeze the name of the anonymous author of antigovernment broadsides out of their printer, John Peter Zenger. A Perry Mason–style courtroom drama ensued, resulting in Zenger's instant release from jail in the name of the freedom of speech of anonymous writers. (In my view, that's when the American Revolution's seeds were sown.)[41]

Thereafter, as Thomas explains with the gleeful enthusiasm one feels on first discovering this rich polemical tradition, guided by Bernard Bailyn's pathbreaking *The Ideological Origins of the American Revolution*, the anonymous pamphlet was the American revolutionary's weapon of choice, from New Jersey governor William Livingston's writings (his *Independent Reflector* journal of the 1750s is one of the monuments of this tradition), through Madison and Hamilton's *Federalist Papers* under the pseudonym "Publius," up until the pseudonymous newspaper article duel of these two great founders over President Washington's 1793 Neutrality Proclamation. As Livingston put it, Thomas writes, anonymity "encouraged authors to discuss politics without fear of reprisal."[42]

If you think this is a trivial, merely antiquarian consideration, Thomas writes in his *Citizens United* opinion, just look at what actually happened in our own day, when California required disclosure on the Internet of the name, address, and employer of anyone who donated more than $100 to the campaign for Proposition 8, asking for a state constitutional amendment recognizing marriage between only a man and a woman as valid. Prop. 8 opponents posted maps on the web showing where supporters lived, so that gay-marriage zealots could harass them or damage their property, as happened widely. Supporters lost their jobs or had their businesses boycotted or mobbed by angry demonstrators. "Supporters recounted being told: 'Consider yourself lucky. If I had a gun I would have gunned you down along with each and every other supporter,' or 'we have plans for you and your friends,'" Thomas writes. Now, he continues, such tactics have metastasized, with bullies using donor information to preempt free speech by warning potential donors of the harms that will befall them if they contribute to conservative candidates. That's why the *Citizens United* majority is as wrong as the *McConnell* one to hold that "disclosure requirements...impose no ceiling on campaign-related activities, and do not prevent anyone from speaking."[43]

———

IN HIS 2005 DISSENT in *Kelo v. New London*, Thomas provides a case study of the process by which the Wilsonian notion of a living, Darwinian Constitution turned the framers' Constitution upside down, interpreting it to mean the polar opposite of what the framers actually wrote. Here are the facts: Five years earlier, the frayed Connecticut city of New London had conceived a grandiose project to redevelop 90 waterfront acres, in tandem with pharmaceutical giant Pfizer's plan to build an adjoining $300 million research center. A conference hotel—that inevitable (and inevitably uneconomic) nostrum of urban economic development schemes—would rise, surrounded by upscale housing, shops, and restaurants, all adorned with a marina and a riverside promenade. Promising to create more than 3,000 new jobs and add $1.2 million to the city's declining tax rolls, the redevelopment authority began buying up the old and modest private houses on the site.

When several longtime owners refused to part with their much-loved homes and water views, the city seized their property under its eminent domain power. Led by resident Susette Kelo, the homeowners (including one who'd lived in her house since 1918) sued the city, claiming that its action violated the Fifth Amendment's guarantee that no person shall "be deprived of life, liberty, or property, without due process of law; nor shall private property be taken for public use, without just compensation." After an appeals court overturned the trial court's ruling in Kelo's favor, the U.S. Supreme Court upheld the city's seizure, 5–4.

Thomas strenuously dissented, based on "the Framers' understanding that property is a natural, fundamental right" that doesn't come from government but inheres in the nature of man. Government exists precisely to protect, not invade, that right. The framers understood that sometimes government would need to acquire private property "when necessary and proper to the exercise of an enumerated power," writes Thomas—to build lighthouses or forts, for example. But they envisioned such taking of property "only if the public has a right to employ it, not if the public realizes any conceivable benefit from the taking," and only if the owner consents and the government pays for it essentially what any private buyer would pay, as William Blackstone had stipulated in his 1760s *Commentaries on the Laws of England*, the standard founding-era legal textbook.

Under no circumstances did the founders imagine that the Fifth Amendment would allow government to "take property away from A. and give it to B.," as New London intends to do with the houses of Kelo and her neighbors, Thomas argues. "The takings clause is a prohibition, not a grant of power." It is an "express limit on the power of the government over the individual," since government exists for the individual's sake, not vice versa.

The federal government, in fact, didn't employ eminent domain power in the early republic, Thomas notes, though the state governments used it "to provide quintessentially public goods," such as roads, canals, and gristmills, which for just compensation could use eminent domain to acquire surrounding land for ponds to power their waterwheels in return for serving the public for a set toll. Some states stretched the mill acts that authorized such enterprises to include private manufacturing plants—a development that champions of eminent domain for purposes other than strictly public use often cite as precedent. But this development drew heavy criticism as being unconstitutional throughout the nineteenth century, Thomas recounts.

One luminous example he might have cited is the objection of the nation's retired first chief justice, John Jay, to an 1812 proposal to take by eminent domain some fields near his Westchester farm and flood them for a private millpond. "When a piece of ground is wanted for a use important to the State, I know that the State has a right to take it from the owner, on paying the full value of it; but certainly the Legislature has no right to compel a freeholder to part with his land to any of his fellow-citizens, nor to deprive him of the use of it, in order to accommodate one or more of his neighbours in the prosecution of their particular trade or business," Jay wrote. "Such an act, by violating the rights of property, would be a most dangerous precedent." As for flooding the fields: "It may be said that the pond, by facilitating manufactures, will be productive of good to the public; but will it not produce more loss than gain, if any of the essential rights of freemen are to be sunk in it?"[44]

In 1896, as the Progressive movement took shape, the Supreme Court began to muddle the issue in earnest in *Fallbrook Irrigation District* v. *Bradley*. In this complex, idiosyncratic case, involving property seized for refusal to pay a tax to build a San Diego County irrigation project and levied only on those who could be directly benefited by it—the landowner thought it unjust to tax her for something she didn't want and wouldn't use—the Court repeatedly conflated the terms "public use" and "public purpose." Doubtless an engineering project that made a desert bloom, enriching not just some of the specific landowners to be taxed but perhaps the entire state economy, is a public boon. Today, in fact, that patch of desert calls itself the Avocado Capital of the World. But public use? Not really, despite the *Fallbrook* Court's pronouncement that the "use must be regarded as a public use, or else it would seem to follow that no general scheme of irrigation can be formed or carried into effect."[45] It could, of course: just let the state's voters approve the project, as with any other public-works bond issue, rather than levy an assessment on particular property owners, as in this case.

Justice John Paul Stevens, writing for the Court in *Kelo*, cited this case with approval for broadening beyond recognition the "use by the public" criterion for takings—a criterion, he said, with true Wilsonian audacity, that was "impractical given the diverse and always evolving needs of society." Even so, objected the more modest Thomas, "the Constitution does not embody those policy preferences."

But *Fallbrook* was nothing compared with what followed. Stevens's *Kelo* opinion cites a 1954 precedent that imperiously wielded the "public purpose" rationale for eminent domain to justify urban renewal projects that tore down vast swathes of supposedly blighted Washington, D.C., property in order to turn the land over to private developers of better housing. Even if you grant the constitutionality of the new rationale, argued the petitioner in this case—who owned a prospering, emphatically unblighted department store within the redevelopment area—creating a "better balanced, more attractive community" was not a valid public purpose. Wrong, said the Supremes, in Justice Douglas's trademark fatuously whimsical language: the legislature, invoking values that are "spiritual as well as physical, aesthetic as well as monetary," has the power "to determine that the community should be beautiful as well as healthy, spacious as well as clean, well-balanced as well as carefully patrolled." Nor need officials deal with property owners on an individual basis in imposing their aesthetic vision on already existing property, so the department store owner's liberty and property rights can claim no protection whatever from the redevelopment juggernaut.[46]

But as Thomas observes of this case in his *Kelo* dissent, "If the slums at issue were truly 'blighted,' then state nuisance law, not the power of eminent domain, would provide the appropriate remedy." And he goes on to note that Justice Douglas's rationale had an unhappy legacy, for under its authority, urban renewal came to mean Negro removal.

The *Kelo* Court also cited another precedent, appropriately from 1984, that is hard to distinguish from a Communist-imposed land reform scheme. Because the government owned 49 percent of Hawaii's land and 72 private landlords owned another 47 percent of it, the state legislature passed a law using eminent domain to wrest the private property from its owners and force them to sell it to their lessees, for just compensation. The Supreme Court blessed this mega-taking's "public purpose": namely, "eliminating the 'social and economic evils of a land oligopoly.'" If only Madison—or George Washington, in his day the nation's biggest landowner—could have opined on the Hawaii legislature's property redistribution edict and the Supreme Court that ratified so "improper or wicked" a takings scheme.[47]

How can the Court so tenderly require the strictest scrutiny to protect such "nontraditional property interests" as welfare benefits, Thomas asks, when it so casually stands aside when a city "invades individuals' traditional rights in real property"? How can it cite "'the overriding respect for the sanctity of the home that has been embedded in our traditions since the origins of the Republic,' when the issue is only whether the government may search a home," and yet supinely say in *Kelo* that "the government may take the infinitely more intrusive step of tearing down petitioners' homes[?] Something has gone seriously awry with this Court's interpretation of the Constitution. Though citizens are safe from the government in their homes, the homes themselves are not." By essentially abolishing the public use clause, the Court has subordinated individual rights to the arbitrary will of the government, Thomas remonstrated. "I do not believe that this Court can eliminate liberties expressly enumerated in the Constitution."[48]

Of course New London's real "public purpose" in taking away Susette Kelo's little pink house and giving her land to the redevelopment authority to sell to private developers was the indirect one of raising the city's tax base. On this rationale, government could order any property razed for higher-value construction, sweeping away single-family houses (especially humble ones) for apartment buildings, churches for stores, or small businesses for national chains. And, Thomas might have added, it makes government officials interested, rather than neutral, parties, since more tax revenue means better pay, health insurance, and pensions for them.

As it happened, getting rid of Kelo's house—ultimately, New London moved it from its waterfront site rather than demolish it—produced loss to all, starting with the lost rights of freemen. In the wake of a merger, Pfizer moved its research facility elsewhere; the redevelopment agency couldn't raise the necessary financing for the rest of the project, which Pfizer's withdrawal rendered problematic; and the land sits vacant, generating not a nickel of tax revenue.

The founders worried constantly about how their envisioned republic might get hijacked, especially by ambitious officials who would transform it into an elective despotism. This is what they meant.

———

ANY DISCUSSION of the Supreme Court in our era must sooner or later come to *Roe* v. *Wade* and abortion. Here is one such procedure, as Nurse Brenda Shafer described it to a congressional committee in 1995—and as Thomas quotes her in his painfully powerful dissent in *Stenberg* v. *Carhart* five years later. After dilating the patient's cervix, the abortionist pulled the 16-week-old fetus by its feet into the vaginal canal, its head still stuck in the uterus, its limbs emerging from the patient's body. "The baby's little fingers were clasping and unclasping, and his little feet were kicking," Shafer testified. "Then the doctor stuck the scissors in the back of his head, and the baby's arms jerked out, like a startle reaction,...like a baby does when he thinks he is going to fall. The doctor opened up the scissors, stuck a high-powered suction tube into the opening, and sucked the baby's brains out. Now the baby went completely limp."

The Court wants to overturn a Nebraska ban on partial-birth abortion? Thomas inquires in *Stenberg*. Then let's look squarely at what we are talking about. Given *this* reality, the "question whether States have a legitimate interest in banning the procedure does not require additional authority. In a civilized society, the answer is too obvious."

But his dissent keeps piling up the cold facts, like George Orwell's insistence on the duty of a constant struggle to see what's in front of one's nose, rather than pretending it's not there or is something different. In another standard second- or third-trimester abortion method, the doctor will dilate the woman's cervix, grab a fetal arm or leg with forceps, and "basically tear off pieces of the fetus and pull them out," a doctor testified. The baby dies from loss of blood. When only the head is left, the doctor will collapse it and pull it out. You are left, the doctor concluded, with a "tray full of pieces." If the fetus presents headfirst, the doctor reverses the procedure. Here in these disjointed parts are Justice Douglas's emanations and penumbras—too, too solid flesh.

But in *Stenberg*, the Court majority "holds that states cannot constitutionally prohibit a method of abortion that millions find hard to distinguish from infanticide and that the Court hesitates even to describe," Thomas writes—because to describe is to condemn. Even *Roe*, which forbade the state from interfering with first-trimester abortions, recognized that *some* regulation could be legal in second- and third-trimester procedures, and that the life of the fetus counts for something, however undefined. While a string of subsequent lower-court decisions inexorably struck down those regulations, until virtually none remained, the Supreme Court stopped the slide to utterly unregulated abortion with *Webster* v. *Reproductive Health Services* in 1989 and especially *Planned Parenthood* v. *Casey*, which, even while upholding *Roe*, ruled in 1992 "that the government has a legitimate and substantial interest in preserving and promoting fetal life" and that states could impose such minimal conditions as a 24-hour waiting period or parental (though not spousal) notification, as long as they did not place a "substantial obstacle in the path of a woman seeking an abortion before the fetus attains viability."[49] But now, with *Stenberg*, Thomas protests, anything goes, even in the third trimester and not excluding virtual infanticide. "It is clear that the Constitution does not compel this result."[50] For that matter, he correctly emphasized in *Gonzales* v. *Carhart*, the 2007 decision that upheld Congress's 2003 ban on partial-birth abortions, all of "the Court's abortion jurisprudence, including *Casey* and *Roe* v. *Wade*, has no basis in the Constitution."[51] (Not that late-term abortions have ended: doctors now work around *Gonzales* by killing the baby while it is still in the womb.)[52]

———

THESE OPINIONS, Thomas's best, add up to a sweeping critique of what the Court, sitting as a Wilsonian permanent constitutional convention and legislating from the bench with ample audacity over seven decades, has wrought. It is not the inspiring panorama of progress that Wilson promised. Commerce Clause jurisprudence has gone far to convert a limited into an unlimited federal government, and the Court-sanctioned expansion of the administrative state has overwhelmed the separation of powers and checks and balances that the founders erected to forestall such a development. The result is that, little by little, although we have kept the name of a self-governing republic, we are losing the actuality, as our unelected bureaucratic servants increasingly become our masters and bind us in their web of rules. Our local communities, once vibrantly self-governing, have lost vital autonomy, as the Court has hemmed in their ability to police themselves and regulate their schools, all in the name of atoning for America's original sin of slavery but in fact harming black Americans more than helping them. So too the race-conscious remedies that the Court has sanctioned or imposed have increased social tensions and distorted key civic institutions. Those liberties that the framers thought so absolute that they enshrined them in the Bill of Rights— freedom of speech, especially political speech, and the protection of private property—became negotiable, with the connivance of a Court established above all to protect those constitutional liberties that it would be tyranny to abridge. It's a strange conception of liberty when we argue over the right to kill our babies.

Intellectually in thrall to his Hegelian mentors, President Wilson imagined History to be the ongoing "realization" of human freedom, in the double sense of becoming real and becoming recognized, and he envisioned an activist Court as History's handmaiden or midwife. For Thomas, the opposite proposition is true. America's Founding Fathers had devised, in the Constitution, history's most perfect guarantor of freedom. All efforts by an activist Court to undo their great work is not progress but vandalism, leading to serfdom. But it is vandalism that we can repair.

CHAPTER FIVE

"A Free Man"

Scarcely two months after Thomas joined the Court, retired African American appellate chief judge A. Leon Higginbotham Jr. ambushed him with a law review piece, "An Open Letter to Justice Clarence Thomas from a Federal Judicial Colleague." So condescending and demeaning is the article, so inappropriate its tone of weary correction, as if addressed to a hopelessly obtuse and refractory pupil, that it's hard not to feel indignation on Thomas's behalf. "Candidly," Higginbotham wrote, "I do not believe that you were indeed the most competent person to be on the Supreme Court"—so far from it, in fact, that a fellow black lawyer is safe to bet that "not one of the senators who voted to confirm Clarence Thomas would hire him as their lawyer." The implied slur: he's just an underqualified affirmative-action appointee. But there he is, and it's "important to remember how you arrived where you are now, because you did not get there by yourself."[1]

How ungrateful, therefore, for Thomas to have complained to the press in 1984 that the black civil rights establishment did nothing but "bitch, bitch, bitch, moan and moan, whine and whine," about the problems of black Americans rather than work with the Reagan administration to solve them, Higginbotham lectured. Didn't he realize that if it were not for such groups as the NAACP, which opened opportunity to blacks through a century's worth of civil rights lawsuits, Thomas himself would be a laborer in Pinpoint today?[2] Without the NAACP's "lobbying, picketing, protesting, and politicking," he would never have gotten out of Georgia, never have gotten into Holy Cross or Yale Law. For that, he should especially thank *Brown v. Board of Education*, which—for all his criticism of the decision, of the Warren Court that issued it, and of Thurgood Marshall who argued it—"recast the racial mores of America" to make a career like Thomas's possible.

That same NAACP led the battle for black voting rights, with the result that the 13 Southern senators who voted to confirm Thomas (a quarter of the 52 yea votes) pushed him over the top because they dared not offend their many black constituents by rejecting a black Supreme Court nominee. It's a long way from the days when Senator Tillman—yes, Pitchfork Ben again—could respond to Theodore Roosevelt's famous White House lunch with Booker T. Washington by hissing, as Higginbotham quotes him, "Now that Roosevelt has eaten with that nigger Washington, we shall have to kill a thousand niggers to get them back to their place."

Then Higginbotham grew still more offensively personal. He had searched out pictures of Thomas's house "in a comfortable Virginia neighborhood," he noted. Had the NAACP not gone to court repeatedly to end residential segregation and discrimination, "you would not be able to live in your own house." And even then, had not the Warren Court struck down Virginia's anti-miscegenation law, Thomas and his white second wife couldn't live there. If they tried, Higginbotham pontificated, "you could have been in the penitentiary today rather than serving as an Associate Justice of the United States Supreme Court."

Given that Thomas has "a stunted knowledge of history and an unformed judicial philosophy," he must "reflect more deeply on legal history than you ever have before," now that he has ascended to the high court, Higginbotham instructs, all but wagging a finger. And what he will find when he does so is that all the great justices, including those Warren Court giants, "viewed the Constitution as an instrument of justice," licensing them to choose which values "to sanction into law." They realized, as Justice Thurgood Marshall put it, that its meaning wasn't forever fixed at the 1787 convention but rather has undergone a *"promising evolution* through 200 years of history," which has uplifted "the disadvantaged, women, minorities, and the powerless."

Packed into this letter are bushels of notions that Thomas hates, from the imputation of inferiority and the charge that he didn't earn the position he holds to the assertions that Supreme Court justices deal with equity, not law, and that the Constitution doesn't have a meaning fixed at the 1787 convention but rather evolves in accordance with the values of the judges who interpret—that is, manufacture—it, by any means necessary, as in *Brown.*

———

So WHEN the National Bar Association, America's foremost convocation of black lawyers and judges, asked him to address its 1998 Memphis convention on the thirtieth anniversary of Martin Luther King's death in that city—and after Judge Higginbotham had doubled down on his insulting letter by warning the group's leaders that inviting Thomas was akin to asking Alabama governor George Wallace to speak fresh from barring the state university door to black students—Thomas accepted the invitation and used the occasion implicitly to answer the older African American judge's screed of six and a half years earlier.

This is a speech worth watching on video for its full emotional impact—the seriousness of the dignified introducer, the grave hush of the attentive audience, the controlled passion of the speaker—earnest, truth-telling, self-revealing, freighted with the *lacrimae rerum*—the tragic sense of life and of history.[3] He knows that having him as a speaker has sparked sharp controversy, and he thanks the organizers for their courage in withstanding it. He knows that many in the audience don't agree with him and view him with suspicion, even hostility. And he wants to tell them that "[i]t pains me...more deeply than any of you can imagine, to be perceived by so many members of my race as doing them harm. All the sacrifice, all the long hours of preparation, were to help, not to hurt."

Like many in the room, he can remember exactly where he was that April 1968 moment when news of Dr. King's shooting reached him. For all of them, the trauma of the event was transformative. "For so many of us who were trying hard to do what we thought was required of us in the process of integrating this society, the rush of hopelessness and isolation was immediate and overwhelming," he recalled, so much so that it "shattered my faith in my religion and my country.... I had accepted the loneliness that came with being 'the integrator,' the first and the only. But this event, this trauma, I could not take." All the other events of the waning 1960s—the murder of Robert Kennedy, the stench of racism, the protest marches, the riots—made him "one angry young man waiting on the revolution that I was certain would come.... All seemed to be defined by race. We became a reaction to the 'man,' his ominous reflection."

Then came the Harvard Square riot. "It was intoxicating to act upon one's rage, to wear it on one's shoulder, to be defined by it. Yet ultimately it was destructive, and I knew it. So in the spring of 1970, in a nihilistic fog, I prayed that I'd be relieved of the anger and the animosity that ate at my soul.... I had to make a fundamental choice. Do I believe in the principles of this country or not? After such angst, I concluded that I did," though the old rage never wholly vanished.

He accepted a complex identity. "I am a man, a black man, an American." Of course he understands "the comforts and security of racial solidarity." But "one of the advantages of growing up in a segregated neighborhood was that we were richly blessed with the ability to see the individuality of each black person with all its fullness and complexity." Now that nuanced understanding has gone out of fashion. Though formerly "we opposed the notion that we all looked alike and talked alike," today "we have come to exalt the new black stereotype above all and to demand conformity to the norm," as if "our race defines us."

Nowhere is conformity more strictly enforced than in the realm of thought. We "establish the range of our thinking and our opinions ... by our color." Not only is this "nothing short of a denial of our humanity," but also it's not thought. "As thinking, rational individuals, not one of us can claim infallibility"; all ideas demand scrutiny "in the realm of reason, not as some doctrinal or racial heresy." Nevertheless, the "particularly bilious and venomous assaults" that have been launched at Thomas— surely Higginbotham is foremost in his mind—imply that "I have no right to think the way I do because I'm black." White people may hold such opinions with impunity; for blacks to hold them, regardless of their truth, is illegitimate.

So that's why he came to Memphis—"to assert my right to think for myself, to refuse to have my ideas assigned to me as though I was an intellectual slave because I'm black. I come to state that I'm a man, free to think for myself and do as I please.... I will not be consigned the unquestioned opinions of others." One can't but honor this as a statement of moral and intellectual heroism on a par with Luther's "Here I stand: I can do no other!" This is what freedom means.

Such an assertion makes Thomas not just an atypical black man but also an atypical American of our time. He sounds more like James Madison than James Baldwin—the Madison driven into politics by anger over his native Virginia's jailing of Baptist preachers for voicing religious opinions differing only slightly from the dogma of the state's established Anglican church. Who ever dreamed of "making laws for the human mind"? Madison raged. As an undergraduate, he had thrilled to the fire-breathing 1750s journal that helped sow the Revolution's Lockean seeds, William Livingston's challengingly named *Independent Reflector*. Thomas, every inch an independent reflector, stands in that tradition.[4]

———

THE POINT of all this is a sweeping and unfamiliar one: it takes a certain kind of character to be capable of, and to cherish, the liberty that the Constitution protects. Thomas himself has made this argument forcefully. His grandfather brought him up aiming to stamp him with just that independent spirit, in as deliberate (and more successful) an experiment in child-rearing as James Mill's early education of his son, John Stuart Mill. Grandfather Anderson shielded his grandson from the surrounding culture almost as completely as if he had been brought up in a pioneer settlement in a vanished era. He had the boy convert from the Southern Baptist church of his birth to orderly Catholicism, sent him to Catholic schools (which made him quick to grasp Jefferson's assertion of God-given rights), put him to work in his small business to instill a powerful work ethic and keep him safe from street culture, and kept him farming all summer long. He taught him to be self-reliant, respectful, resolute, and equipped with a moral maxim for every foreseeable adversity.

That adversity would appear was a given in segregated Savannah, but "the very notion of submitting to one's circumstances was unthinkable" in his grandparents' house, the justice recalls. Thomas and his brother couldn't hint "that difficult circumstances could prevail over individual effort" without cueing one of Grandfather Anderson's stock maxims—"Where there's a will, there's a way," perhaps. "Overcoming adversity not only gives us our measure as individuals," Thomas reflects, "but it also reinforces those basic principles and rules without which a society based upon freedom and liberty cannot function."[5] And the first of those rules is that you have "to accept both the responsibilities and the consequences of personal freedom." For the "dirty little secret of freedom" is that, in many respects, "you're on your own. You're crossing the prairie of life at your own risk," just like the American pioneers.[6] No wonder Thomas loves to quote the charge of Thomas à Kempis—as much Stoic as Christian—"to ensure that in every place, action, and outward occupation you remain inwardly free and your own master. Control circumstances, and do not allow them to control you. Only so can you be a master and ruler of your actions, not their servant or slave; a free man."[7]

Experience and example, more than maxims, went into the making of Thomas. Those dawn-to-dusk summer days on the farm taught him self-reliance by making him rely on himself, in this instance for life's basic needs. "I wouldn't say we were off the grid, but we were never on the grid," he said in a 2018 talk. "We were in a grid-free zone."[8] He learned how to raise and butcher a pig; plant, nurture, harvest, and store crops; build a house from cinder blocks he helped make himself; and cooperate with his family to accomplish all this. Unlike the majority of Americans, his family had not outsourced—or alienated, a Marxist philosopher might say—fundamental life skills to faceless others. They did not depend on "society" but on themselves, like the sturdy yeomen of Thomas Jefferson's telling. In the process, Thomas found that self-reliance breeds self-confidence.

"One of my favorite memories of my grandfather is how he would walk slowly by the corn field, admiring the fruits of his labor," Thomas reminisced in a 1995 speech. "I have often thought that just the sight of a tall stand of corn must have been more nourishing to his spirit than the corn itself was to his body." *The fruits of his labor*, literally—and helping to bring them forth from what had been fallow ground fed his grandson's soul, too.[9]

Toward the end of his grandfather's life, Thomas asked him why he insisted on running his own then-declining business, an all-day, every-day affair for not much money, rather than work 40 or 50 hours a week for a bigger company in a secure job. "It's *mine*," his grandfather replied. As Thomas recounted in a 1993 speech, "That trumped security. Secretly, I think he just couldn't stand the idea of anyone telling him what to do or where to go. For that freedom, he was willing to accept the other side—the anxiety and the work. In fact, he seemed to relish the challenge of being successfully independent and thus free."[10]

———

AMERICA'S FOUNDING FATHERS radiated this spirit of liberty. They had hopes, but no illusions, that the Constitution they wrote to safeguard individual freedom would be eternal. To preserve the unexampled free republic they created would require something more: a culture of liberty—a belief throughout the whole people in the values that sustain freedom. Should "listlessness for the preservation of natural and unalienable rights" ever infect Americans, George Washington had warned, then "no mound of parchment can be so formed as to stand against the sweeping torrent of boundless ambition on the one side, aided by the sapping current of corrupted morals on the other."[11]

As Justice Thomas puts it, "I think today we think that all the work is done with the laws." But that isn't true for his own sense of free American citizenship. "The heavy lifting for us was done in *here*"—putting his finger on his heart—"because the people who raised us believed it in *here*. The nuns who taught us believed it in *here*."[12]

But the cultural infection that George Washington feared ultimately set in, and Thomas proposes two theories of how it happened, with unhappy consequences for both individual and national American character. The first theory emphasizes the power of culture. We used to venerate heroes, Thomas says—men like Washington or Lincoln or George Washington Carver. People of his generation (and mine) grew up reading biographies of them—books aimed at youngsters and stressing that the great deeds of the father of his country, for instance, flowed directly from the virtues of his character, especially his integrity and work ethic, which allowed him to become a self-made hero. So we learned both that history and progress are made by great individuals, and that, if we are ambitious to excel, we should cultivate virtue. Even if, more modestly, we aim merely to succeed, we should emulate "the courage, persistence, discipline, hard work, [and] humility" of Horatio Alger's orphan newsboy, for example, who could "triumph in the face of adversity."[13]

That understanding evaporated as the 1950s ended, Thomas argues. A new furor for equality seized American culture and generated a distaste for heroic excellence. Biographers began deconstructing heroes, looking for flaws and follies (the more lurid, the better), in "a conscious attempt to cheapen their achievements." Obsessions, neuroses, or base passions—"self-interest, revenge, self-aggrandizement, insecurity"—replaced virtue as the supposed motive force for great deeds, which most likely came about by a lucky accident rather than an intent to do good. Historians who tout equality, Thomas quotes Alexis de Tocqueville as saying, generally depict history as made by vast external forces, not great men, and they "take away from the people themselves the faculty of modifying their own lot and make them depend on an inflexible providence or a kind of blind fatality," which implicitly denies the possibility of self-government.

America's veneration of heroes gave way to a preoccupation with victims, Thomas notes. That shift occurred partly because of a growing belief in the irresistible power of those vast external forces that Tocqueville mentions. "Many argued that human actions and choices, like events in the natural world, are often caused by factors beyond one's control," Thomas wrote in *City Journal*. People increasingly took for granted that such mighty determinisms as social injustice or 400 years of slavery and racism ineluctably shape individual fate today. Against these, the individual has no defense. He can only be the victim of such circumstances, not the master of them.

That change in cultural assumptions went hand in hand with an altered view of the relation of the individual citizen to the government, the second of Thomas's explanations for the waning of America's culture of liberty and the independent individual character that it nurtured and was in turn nurtured by. For the founders, government's purpose was the protection of the individual's liberty to pursue his own happiness in his own way, according to his own tastes and talents. How he used that liberty was his own responsibility, as were the ensuing consequences. But what if external circumstances were the real cause of his actions? What if he was *driven* to do what he did, rather than choosing it? Is he still accountable? "Many began to hesitate to hold responsible those whose conduct might be explained as a response to societal injustice," Thomas observes. "[O]thers questioned how we could tell blacks in our inner cities to face the consequences of breaking the law when the very legal system—and indeed the society—that will judge their conduct has perpetuated years of racism and unequal treatment under the law."[14]

So American culture's faith in the justness of the state's primary obligation—to give citizens the basic civil right of being safe in their homes and in the streets—wavered. Government tied down law enforcement with as many procedural rules as the cords the Lilliputians used to bind Gulliver, and (except for New York's second golden age, under Mayors Giuliani and Bloomberg) policed ghettoes lackadaisically, in the guilt-ridden sense that the criminal was really the victim—of racism, privation, injustice, or lack of opportunity. Perhaps he acted out of justified rage at the wrongs that a racist society had heaped upon him—the kind of rage that Thomas felt at the Harvard Square riot and immediately rejected as soul-destroying.

But look at what happens when government and society stop holding people accountable for their actions. If we are squeamish about punishing criminals, or evicting dope pushers from public housing, or suspending knife-toting kids from public schools, we create an environment in which right-doing citizens can't go to work without fear, and kids who want to succeed can't get educated. Perhaps worse, if we don't condemn and punish wrongdoers, we tell the law-abiding that their behavior is no more praiseworthy than the criminal's or the delinquent's. As Thomas puts it, "the law cannot persuade where it cannot punish."[15]

The New Deal, Thomas argues, marked an inflection point in government's subversion of personal responsibility. FDR's promise of freedom from want, in particular, redefined freedom from "a right to self-provision and self-determination" to "a right to make demands on government and society for one's well-being and happiness," for housing, a minimum income, and other such benefits. The Supreme Court's 1970 *Goldberg v. Kelly* decision marks the *reductio ad absurdum* of the New Deal idea that a benevolent state can eliminate or remedy adversity and misfortune—"a fundamental misreading of the human condition," Thomas thinks. That decision defined cash welfare payments as an entitlement, a kind of property right—not a privilege—and government couldn't end them without a due process hearing, complete with the right to counsel.[16] In other words, the government owes you a living. It's not your responsibility to make your own, or your fault if you don't.[17] And with 2016 census data showing that 52 percent of Americans under 18 live in a household where at least one member receives a means-tested government benefit, Thomas's sweeping statement seems like prophecy.[18]

Affirmative action proved yet one more solvent of the culture of liberty. You can't earn praise or blame for the consequences of your pursuit of your own happiness in your own way if government or institutions rig the game for or against you, any more than if vast impersonal forces are arrayed to stymie you. But that's what affirmative action does. It substitutes social engineering for merit, obstructing your freedom to mold your own fate. Like the failure to punish wrongdoers, it denies that there is better and worse, higher and lower. There is just "equal," by design. In affirmative action, individuals are the toys of an arbitrary government or arbitrary institutions, rather than captains of their own soul. This is hardly a medium that nurtures heroes, and it certainly doesn't sustain an inventive, entrepreneurial society.

The cumulative result of these transvaluations of values is catastrophic. While it's true that people do right because they are afraid of the worst consequences of doing wrong—jail or failure—the more powerful reason is that they have a right-doing character. They do right because they know it *is* right. Conscience is stronger than the cops. "In the long run," Thomas says, "a society that abandons personal responsibility will lose its moral sense."

Worse, "the acceptance of diminished responsibility shackle[s] the human spirit from rising above the tragedies of one's condition."[19] Here is the nub of the issue. Government and society stand in a dialectical relationship with individual character. Changes in one side of the equation precipitate changes in the other, and that new alteration sparks changes in the first term, as government and character mutually modify each other. Only citizens who believe that they are free to mold their circumstances are capable of self-government—of freedom. A free government depends on citizens who believe themselves able to pursue their happiness in their own way, taking responsibility for the outcome. And the reverse is true. To believe you are unfree, bound and shaped by circumstance, is a self-fulfilling prophecy, resulting in a servile state. To put it another way, as people lose their veneration for the unalienable rights of mankind and their reverence for the active, heroic virtues that sustain them, the rights themselves crumble, government looms larger, the people feel themselves all the more powerless and dependent, allowing government to arrogate ever more power to itself, and so on, in a vicious circle.

———

THOMAS JUMPS so quickly from George Washington to welfare that it's worth pausing to fill in the gap, the better to grasp the key point about character and freedom so crucial to understanding him. His mention of Tocqueville, the brilliant author of *Democracy in America*, provides the needed clue. Based on the aristocratic French lawyer's nine months crisscrossing the young country at age 26 in 1831, from New England south to New Orleans and west to the virgin forests around Lake Superior, interviewing everyone from President Andrew Jackson to the last of the Iroquois, *Democracy* is not only an insightful account of American exceptionalism and a prophetic critique of American democracy's shortcomings; it is also a profound meditation on the interrelationship of character and government.

Democracy, Tocqueville saw in America, gives rise to "a manly and legitimate passion for equality that spurs all men to wish to be strong and esteemed." Yet it can also lead weak men "to want to bring the strong down to their level"—with such fervor as ultimately to defeat democracy's purpose by "preferring equality in servitude to inequality in freedom." That's why the shift in focus from heroes to victims that Justice Thomas rues is so easy. Nor do American equality and materialism provide fertile ground for deep thought. As people increasingly resemble each other, each man intellectually "feels weaker vis à vis all the others" and "loses confidence in himself when they combat him." Public opinion bears all before it—so irresistibly that Tocqueville can think of "no country where there is in general less independence of mind and true freedom of discussion than in America."[20] Democracy, one might say, depends for its creation on independent reflectors, such as America's fiercely self-examining Puritan settlers, but, once established, it doesn't nurture them.

With no need for the racks and chains of old, democracy's very mild tyranny "ignores the body and goes straight for the soul," Tocqueville laments. It leaves the dissident his life, liberty, property, and civic privileges, but it makes them useless to him by making him a pariah, unable to gain the esteem or the votes of his fellow citizens, who will shun him for his unorthodox ideas for fear of being shunned themselves. So while formal political independence still exists, the loss of intellectual independence waters it down, the letter without the spirit. If you want a refutation of the wisdom of crowds—the "theory of equality applied to intelligence," Tocqueville scoffs—look no further. As someone who believes that "freedom of the intellect is a sacred thing," as Tocqueville does, "when I feel the hand of power weigh upon my brow, it scarcely matters who my oppressor is, and I am not more inclined to submit to the yoke because a million arms are prepared to place it around my neck."[21] You can see why Justice Thomas finds him so congenial.

Part of the genius of the U.S. Constitution—perhaps its strongest barrier to the rise of democratic tyranny, in Tocqueville's view—is that it not only prevents Congress from making laws for localities but it also provides no central administrative system that could carry them out if they existed. Each town is a little republic, with the people governing themselves like homespun Athenians in the direct democracy of the town meeting. American culture nurtures independent self-reliance in practical matters from childhood on. Even in the schoolyard, American children make up their own rules and punish infractions themselves. As adults, they never wait for government to solve everyday problems. If a road gets blocked, they organize themselves to fix it. Spontaneous nongovernmental associations—seminaries, hospitals, temperance unions—spring up for furthering "public security, commerce and industry, morality and religion," Tocqueville marvels. "There is nothing the human will despairs of achieving through the free action of the collective power of individuals."[22] Free and collaborative: that's the mainspring of American mores.

A good thing, because, given the majoritarian tyranny that reigns over U.S. public opinion, a centralized administration would pose a fearful danger. If the central power could issue orders and frame general principles for local communities and also carry them out in detail, if it could reach down and seize the individual by the collar, "then liberty would soon be banished from the New World," Tocqueville asserts.[23]

When he articulated this inspired intuition, Tocqueville had already begun to see, at the start of his 12 years as a French legislator, just how administrative despotism worked in his own nation. From the mid-fifteenth century onward, as he recounts in his 1856 *The Old Regime and the French Revolution*, the French monarchy inexorably centralized power in a handful of top bureaucrats, whose underlings regulated poor relief in every parish, told farmers what they could plant and where, regulated the ancient mediating private and corporate institutions of local self-government (from hospitals and convents to factories and colleges), and set up administrative courts that crowded out the real justice system and provided "an image of justice rather than justice itself."[24] These bureaucrats ensnared the country in a net of regulations; they smothered it with forms to be filled out.[25]

With only 12,000-odd U.S. officials as against France's 138,000 in the 1830s, what a difference America's administrative decentralization makes in the national character. "People care about their country's interests as though they were their own," Tocqueville enthused. "In its successes they see their own work and are exalted by it." By contrast, the French of his day are "indifferent to the fate of the place they live in," and think that the fate of their town and the safety of their streets "have nothing to do with them, that they belong to some powerful stranger called 'the government.'"[26]

But ultimately, as happened in France, a gigantic, centralized modern state grew up inside the shell of America's founding-era institutions, with few Americans even noticing and most unaware of the magnitude of the revolution even today. We created a giant administrative regime, just as Tocqueville feared, composed of the New Deal agencies and their spawn, operating free of the Constitution's checks and balances and outside the Article III justice system. Those 12,000 federal employees have grown to 2.7 million today, not to mention the 14.3 million who man state and local governments. The code of federal regulations now totals some 180,000 pages.

What's more, this Second American Revolution occurred under just the rationale that Tocqueville predicted. Democratic citizens, he wrote, "are willing enough to grant that the power that represents society possesses far more enlightenment and wisdom than any of the men who compose it and that its duty as well as its right is to take each citizen by the hand and guide him."[27] Thus Woodrow Wilson set the administrative state in motion in the name of disinterested government by non-political experts, who would advance the common good so much more efficiently than the free action of the collective power of individuals. Senator Feinstein is parroting his words to this day.

When the New Deal took administrative government to new depths of unconstitutionality, Franklin Roosevelt and his brain trust used almost Tocquevillian language in explaining why, in the age of giant corporations purportedly more powerful than any individual citizen or mediating institution, only an equally mighty government could protect the wee, timorous, cowering individual. "Thus the industrial class needs to be regulated, supervised, and restrained," wrote Tocqueville, "and it is natural for the prerogatives of government to grow along with it." The argument will be, Tocqueville predicted, that "as citizens become weaker and less capable, government must be made more skillful and active, so that society can take upon itself what individuals are no longer capable of doing on their own"—a sentiment that could have come from one of FDR's fireside chats.[28] "Entrenched greed," charged FDR in his 1936 State of the Union speech, "will take the course of every autocracy of the past—power for themselves, enslavement for the public."

Tocqueville couldn't find a precise enough name for the new oppressiveness that he saw coming into being—saw with a shiver, like those who, wondering and secretly afraid, witness the demonic power of an atomic bomb explosion, or like astronauts watching the Earth become an ever smaller blue ball as they hurtle into the silent void, seeing what hitherto only God has seen. "'Despotism' and 'tyranny' will not do." He groped for a description that would adequately convey the almost otherworldly force he glimpsed in outline, a presence like something out of science fiction, human and yet inhuman, shaping the very character—the souls—of individual citizens.[29]

Over today's swarming millions of equal, materialistic, isolated individuals, he wrote, "stands an immense tutelary power, which assumes sole responsibility for securing their pleasure and watching over their fate." This new kind of sovereign, "after taking individuals one by one in his powerful hands and kneading them to his liking," will spread over society "a fine mesh of uniform, minute, and complex rules," which constrain even the best and brightest. "He does not break men's wills but softens, bends, and guides them. He seldom forces anyone to act but consistently opposes action. He does not destroy things but rather prevents them from coming into being. Rather than tyrannize, he inhibits, represses, saps, stultifies, and in the end reduces each nation to nothing but a timid and industrious flock of animals, with the government as its shepherd."[30]

In America, an iron cage of administrative rules arose to prevent new businesses from opening, old ones from hiring, doctors from treating patients as they think best, groups of citizens from uttering political speech, even a landowner from moving a pile of sand from one spot to another on his property, purportedly because it could affect a navigable waterway fifty miles away. It slows projects to a crawl, so that building a bridge, a skyscraper, a power plant takes years, not the mere months it took pre–New Deal America to build the Empire State Building. It pressures men not to speak their minds or say what they see in front of their own eyes but rather to mouth the dogmas of orthodoxy. If some entrepreneur does invent something new—some novel communications technology, as it happens—it serves to make people even more alike and more isolated in the solitude of their own hearts, and the first impulse of the entrepreneur and his Stanford-indoctrinated staff, organization men as conformist as any 1950s junior executive, is to regulate and censor what can be said over it.

Just as the French state co-opted the private hospitals and colleges, so has the immense tutelary power of America's administrative state turned private charities into government contractors, so that Catholic Charities or Jewish Social Services are neither Catholic nor Jewish—though most public welfare comes direct from the state, from babies' milk to old people's health care and pensions, for which only a minority has paid. As Tocqueville observed, "It is the state that has undertaken virtually alone to give bread to the hungry, aid and shelter to the sick, and work to the idle," transforming, as Justice Thomas puts it, the fundamental American ideas of "freedom from government interference into a right to welfare payments."[31] And whatever traditional American mores defined as good and bad, moral and immoral, base and praiseworthy, the sovereign has redefined and redefined until all such ideas have lost their meaning. Is it any wonder that today's Americans feel that they have no say in how they are governed—or that they don't understand how that came about?

Such oppression is "less degrading" in democracies, Tocqueville writes, because, since the citizens elect the sovereign, "each citizen, hobbled and reduced to impotence though he may be, can still imagine that in obeying he is only submitting to himself." Moreover, once democratic citizens come to love equality more than liberty, the love of equality grows as equality itself expands. "The only necessary condition for centralizing public power in a democratic society is to love equality or to make a show of loving it. Thus the science of despotism," Tocqueville despairingly concluded, "can be reduced ... to a single principle."[32]

In modern America, the forces that Tocqueville saw as protections against democratic despotism have flagged, while those that advance it have strengthened. The free and collaborative culture he admired has receded. Instead of making up their own rules and enforcing them on the playground, today's children, overprotected, overprogrammed, and overcontrolled—or else neglected and given over to the culture of the streets and its gangs—don't dependably learn resilience, autonomy, and self-reliance. Adults rarely join together to solve local problems. Instead, the administrative state, sucking the oxygen from the mediating institutions of civil society through which people once made their own decisions about local governance, has turned independent reflectors into timid sheep, unaware of how much of their liberty has vanished.

And the tyranny of public opinion has found a force multiplier in our new version of the quest for equality. Our educational system, from kindergarten through graduate school, now teaches that—on the basis of color, sex, citizenship, or "gender"—we are either victims or victimizers, and our duty, or our right, is to equalize or expiate that which can never be equalized or expiated, because the white or male or heterosexual victimizers constantly inflict violences perceptible only to the victims. These "microaggressions" include statements such as "America is the land of opportunity" or "I believe the most qualified person should get the job," according to the University of California system's top brass.[33] In other words, those who make our culture have redefined the basic American creed into a kind of violence, and they sit on their hands when college mobs shout down or disinvite speakers who dissent. While worrying that robots with artificial intelligence will take away our jobs, we might spare a worry that schools and colleges are turning our kids into robots, with preprogrammed minds that aren't equipped for creativity, individuality, resilience, or liberty.

This is the missing term in Thomas's account of the relation of individual character to free government. It is a dialectic that involves the whole population, not just the poor and minorities. It's that inner capitulation, the refusal to accept or assign personal responsibility for what the individual makes of the liberty that America offers, and thus to devalue the liberty itself, that Thomas despises from the depths of his being. "If you make your bed hard, you lay in it hard," the justice's grandfather told him. "This doesn't sound very compassionate," Thomas reflects, and Grandfather Anderson "often seemed unsympathetic to one's poor use of freedom—that is, if one can call his demand to live up to the responsibilities of freedom and accept the consequences of his actions unsympathetic." But consider: this ferociously proud man in segregated Savannah, where white people presumed to call him "boy," Thomas recalls, "did all he could to preserve his freedom, and to provide the tools for his family [to] secure and maintain their freedom.... It would seem to me that those are the things of legends and heroes."[34]

———

I THINK SO, TOO; and unease about the spiritual capitulation that makes people shrink from the burdens of liberty, and the political consequences of that surrender, sparked this book. Let me explain, briefly, because the book's origin illuminates this key point.

After writing about the memoirs and other works of Barack Obama toward the end of his presidency, I came away disheartened by the tendentiousness of his moral vision and the void at the core of his identity, emptier than most modern politicians. Of course he faced a notoriously vexed challenge in making sense of who he is, as the son of a black Kenyan who deserted him before he was born and a flibbertigibbet white mother, who, like Dickens's Mrs. Jellyby, practiced a "telescopic philanthropy" more concerned about the faraway wretched of the earth than her own children, and who abandoned young Barry for long stretches while she went to uplift the women of Indonesia, her second husband's homeland. Meanwhile, her parents brought up her son.

Both Kansans, Obama's grandparents had opposite temperaments. Grandfather Dunham, a dreamy utopian like Obama's Kumbaya mother, was "always searching for a new start, always running away from the familiar," in a "desire...to obliterate the past" and a "confidence in the possibility of remaking the world from whole cloth," Obama writes.[35] In that spirit, he transplanted his family to the new state of Hawaii, where he drifted from failure to failure. Obama's grandmother, by contrast, had an indomitable character reminiscent of Clarence Thomas's grandfather's, though quieter—so decent and determined that she rose to be one of the Bank of Hawaii's first woman vice presidents. "[H]er dogged practicality," Obama gratefully recalls, "kept the family afloat."[36]

In a family of two white midwesterners in polyglot Hawaii, with few black residents and no blacks in his tony private school until junior high, Obama "was trying to raise myself to be a black man in America," he writes, "and beyond the given of my appearance, no one around me seemed to know what that meant." By hanging around with the University of Hawaii's first-string basketball players, all black ringers from the mainland, the young teen learned both the game and its accompanying cocky attitude, but he secretly feared he was only acting out "a caricature of black male adolescence."[37]

To fill out the picture, he read the African American canon from W.E.B. Du Bois to Malcolm X—an indoctrination in angry victimology, stressing that "being black meant only the knowledge of your own powerlessness, your own defeat," he writes. His newly arrived best friend in junior high, Ray from L.A., scoffed at this earnest search: "I don't need no books to tell me how to be black." Obama got closer to the real McCoy at L.A.'s Occidental College, where he and his fellow radical black students blasted their stereos as aggressively as Clarence Thomas did at Holy Cross, to prove that "we were alienated." Transferring to Columbia, he lived on an as-yet-ungentrified Manhattan block, where, as he thought with fevered racial grievance, "white people from the better neighborhoods nearby walk[ed] their dogs…to let the animals shit on our curbs."[38]

From his first real job, as a community organizer in a Chicago housing project next door to a sewage treatment plant, he drew all the wrong lessons, despite the earnest effort of the African Americans around him to set him straight. In only a generation since the great migration north, they told him, black America had lost its family-transmitted and community-enforced culture of respectability, public decorum, hard work, self-restraint, and belief that education led to opportunity. But Obama concluded, on the contrary, that though culture counts, "culture is shaped by circumstance"—the ultimate determinant—and for African Americans those circumstances came down to "the scars of slavery and Jim Crow, the internalized rage and forced ignorance, the shame of men who could not protect their women or support their families, the children who grew up being told that they wouldn't amount to anything and had no one there to undo the damage" that white America had inflicted. So it's getting the truth exactly backward to claim, as his Chicago friends did no less than conservatives like Thomas, "that cultural pathologies—rather than racism or structural inequalities built into our economy—[are] responsible for black poverty," or "that government programs like welfare, coupled with liberal judges who coddled criminals, actually made those pathologies worse."[39]

The ultimate truth about black identity, he grew ever more certain, was victimhood—"greater deprivation, and hence authenticity." It made no sense to speculate about the tangled relationship of "psychology and politics, the state of our pocketbooks and the state of our souls." Not only too complicated, any analysis of how character interacts with circumstance "demanded too much honest self-reckoning from people," more than Obama would ask of them or of himself—perhaps, in his case, because of the self-doubt that plagues every affirmative-action "beneficiary." For practical purposes, he decided, circumstance trumps character.[40]

Whatever uncertainties that lingered about his own identity vanished when a Florida neighborhood-watch volunteer shot and killed troubled black teen Trayvon Martin, purportedly in self-defense, in 2013. Sweeping aside the tangled ambiguities around the case, President Obama declared, "You know, when Trayvon Martin was first shot, I said that this could have been my son.... Trayvon Martin could have been me 35 years ago." And thereafter he hammered home that message after every isolated incident of a cop shooting a black American justifiably or accidentally, with scarcely a thought for the platoons of inner-city African American youths mowed down by other blacks year in, year out—or for the police officers assassinated by deranged blacks inflamed by his anti-cop demagogy.[41]

This belief, focusing more sharply the race-victimology central to his sense of self, shaped his presidential policy. "All Americans should be troubled by these shootings, because these are not isolated incidents. They're symptomatic of a broader set of racial disparities that exist in our criminal justice system." After all, blacks and Hispanics, "who make up only 30 percent of the general population, make up more than half of the incarcerated population," he wrote. "And when incidents like this occur, there's a big chunk of our fellow citizenry that feels as if because of the color of their skin, they are not being treated the same. And that hurts." How Obama could not have noticed that African Americans murder eight times as frequently as whites and Hispanics combined is a mystery. If black New Yorkers, 23 percent of the city's population, are jailed "disproportionally" to their numbers, that's because they disproportionally commit two-thirds of Gotham's violent crimes. Even so, right up to the end of his presidency, Obama was still trumpeting the black incarceration rate to prove that Americans "have by no means overcome the legacies of slavery and Jim Crow and colonialism and racism," even though they elected him to move the nation into a post-racial future.[42]

But to vindicate the lie at the heart of his sense of self, he did exactly the opposite. He practiced victim politics. On the false assumption that only discrimination can explain any disproportionate representation of blacks anywhere, he loosed his attorneys general to scour the land, like racial grand inquisitors, to expose racism in every cranny of American life, from school discipline, to local zoning in upscale white suburbs, to voter ID laws (though no one charges racism when you must show your ID and more to get on a plane). Attorney General Eric Holder even refused to prosecute the New Black Panther Party's intimidation of white voters by rationalizing that it came nowhere near the intimidation of black would-be voters in Jim Crow days. The administration banned drug tests after traffic crashes, lest they turn up "too many" drug-impaired minority drivers.

To swell the rolls, administration minions found lesser, non-black victims behind every tree, such as the employees of nuns who didn't want to provide them with birth control that their religion considers sinful, or homosexuals for whom a baker refused to make a wedding cake (also for religious reasons), or deadbeats to whom banks were now forced to make loans, or college girls whose charges of rape college administrators were pressured to take at face value without really checking their truth, blighting the lives of bewildered college boys without even a pretense of due process in their disciplinary proceedings.

Moreover, because the federal government had once instituted purportedly universal programs, such as Social Security, that benefited white much more than black Americans (Social Security originally excluded such predominantly black occupations as domestic or agricultural work), Obama's Washington introduced such supposedly universal programs as early-childhood education, higher minimum wages, and Obamacare, designed in fact to benefit minorities more than whites. Minorities, for example, made up a disproportionate share of those lacking health insurance.[43]

The sense of victimhood around which Obama had constructed his self-conception, and which suffused his politics, left no room for the idea of individual agency or even individual free will. Nowhere did he make that assumption more clear than in an oft-quoted 2012 campaign speech: "Look, if you've been successful, you didn't get there on your own," he declared. "If you've got a business—you didn't build that. Somebody else made that happen. The Internet didn't get invented on its own. Government research created the Internet so that all the companies could make money off the Internet." For Obama, as Tocqueville foresaw, the credit for every advance, every success, "belong[s] to some powerful stranger called 'the government.'" Don't think success comes from your special intelligence or hard work, Obama lectured; legions of smart, hardworking people don't have the luck to prosper by fortuitously catching the wave of some vast force reshaping the world. Even so, it takes a village. Thank the government for providing the teacher who encouraged you, for the roads and bridges that bring your goods to market. And finally, thank the unnamed agents who "helped to create this unbelievable American system that we have that allowed you to thrive"—and if you think he has the heroes at Valley Forge and the Constitutional Convention in mind, rather than FDR, his brain trust, and his bureaucrats, who "sav[ed] capitalism from itself through an activist federal government that invests in people and infrastructure, regulates the marketplace, and protects labor from chronic deprivation" through the welfare state, think again. And add in, for good measure, a Constitution that is "not a static but rather a living document, and must be read in the context of an ever-changing world."[44]

The individual victim, tempest-tossed by circumstances he cannot master; the collectivist state as the shepherd of Tocqueville's timid and (sometimes) industrious flock, whether to protect them from injustice or direct their activities, which, were they left to their own devices, would produce nothing; the wise administrators whose far-seeing eyes discern the arc of history's direction and can guide their flock accordingly: after weeks of living with this vision, I felt suffocated, soiled, needing something to sweeten my imagination.

———

JUST BY CHANCE, my eye fell upon Clarence Thomas's memoir, forgotten on the shelf where I'd put it in 2008, after he had kindly inscribed it for me. It reminded me of a morning I'd spent with the justice in 1995. The vivid recollection of his direct, openhearted talk about real, lived experience—his infectious laughter at the follies of the world and our own youth, including its race politics—made me think I might have found the antidote I wanted. And so it proved.

"There is nothing you can do to get past black skin," Thomas told Juan Williams in 1987; "you'll never be seen as equal to whites."[45] But then what? You have a choice. As I read the memoir—to invoke once more Thomas's self-identification as "a man, a black man, an American"—the black man soon gave way to the American, the independent citizen who thinks for himself, does for himself, relies on himself, and, not incidentally, fights for the right of others to enjoy the same liberties. That certainly seems to have been the trajectory of Thomas's own experience. In a 2012 colloquy at the National Archives with Yale law professor Akhil Reed Amar, the son of Indian immigrants, he remarked, "No one cares that forty years ago you and I would not be sitting here talking about the Constitution of the United States, except to say we're excluded. And now, it's hardly noticed."[46]

"If you've been successful, you didn't get there on your own," Obama lectures, just as Judge Higginbotham lectured Thomas that he had "to remember how you arrived where you are now, because you did not get there by yourself." What is that but a platitude? Of course no man is an island. Of course every innovator stands on the shoulders of giants. Of course we all belong to a society—and, as Thomas says, ours is uniquely rich in individual opportunity and possibility. But as he also insists, each individual is personally responsible for the use he makes of his liberty and the consequences of his pursuit of happiness. In this critical sense, every American is self-made. And as for rising far beyond Pinpoint, as Thomas once said, "My grandfather—that's the guy that got me out. It wasn't all these people who are claiming all this leadership stuff."[47]

Individuals are victims of circumstance, says President Obama, not masters of them? Tell that to the colonists who hewed America out of wilderness and fought a war to be free to form a government by reason and reflection, not accident or force. Tell it to Clarence Thomas, who made himself what he is through all the sacrifice, all the long hours of preparation, all the loneliness that came with being "the integrator," the first and the only. How could so fiercely independent a soul, and one who had to fight for his right to be independent, not want to restore a Constitution that protects liberty? Liberty for all, because in his opposition to all the government-made nostrums that have kept blacks dependent, *he* is the black American statesman who is opening the door to our much-longed-for post-racial future.

In our age of enraged shrinking violets, in which hypersensitivity to imagined slights alternates with rage against any nonconformity to orthodoxy, Clarence Thomas is one of a handful of honest and brave iconoclasts who love liberty, especially the freedom to think for oneself, and who know how America, imperfect as all human things are imperfect, nevertheless was uniquely conceived in liberty and dedicated to the proposition that all men are created equal. "I've lived the flaws" of the Constitution, Thomas says, thinking of his early years. "I've lived the contradictions." Nevertheless, "one of the birthrights that's been passed on to me is that I still believe it's perfectible," he says. "When I go into the building that I work in now, that's the theme I try to carry with me and with my clerks: it's perfectible," he remarked in 2013. "It's worth getting up every day and trying to make it right." In fact, he said, "It's like the priesthood: this is what I was called to do."[48]

We marvel that late eighteenth-century America produced its band of great men who invented our republic on such revolutionary principles. It's a marvel that there are some who'd like to restore it as the world's beacon of individual liberty. Through a similarly lucky alchemy of character and culture that nurtured the founders, our age has produced Justice Thomas. Surely it isn't too much to hope that it will produce enough of his ilk to kindle a new birth of freedom.

Acknowledgments

Sincere thanks to the trustees and staff of the Manhattan Institute and the editors of *City Journal* for many years of support and encouragement, including during every stage of the writing of this book. Thanks, too, to the Dian Graves Owen Foundation of Abilene, Texas, for its generous support of the book's production and promotion. I owe a special debt of gratitude to my old friend Peter Reinharz, former chief prosecutor of New York City's family court and more recently a law professor, for sage, practical, and passionate advice—gladly followed—about some of the technical legal matters discussed in chapter 4. Anthony Daniels and Theodore Dalrymple encouraged me to write this book before I had quite intended to and in a shape that I also hadn't quite intended, with satisfying results. Roger Kimball, the polymath chief of Encounter Books, who is every author's dream of an ideal publisher, smoothed away practical difficulties with apparent effortlessness. And my son, Alec Magnet, helped me think through some of the deeper philosophical issues implicit in this book through many intense, absorbing, and genial Sunday dinner conversations.

Notes

CHAPTER ONE: OUR CRISIS OF LEGITIMACY

1   William Cummings, "Hillary Clinton: You 'Cannot Be Civil' with
    Republicans, Democrats Need to Be 'Tougher,'" *USA Today*, 9 October 2018,
    https://www.usatoday.com/story/news/politics/onpolitics/2018/10/09/
    hillary-clinton-cnn-interview/1578636002; Jacqueline Thomsen, "Booker:
    Those Who Don't Oppose Kavanaugh Are 'Complicit in the Evil,'" *The Hill*,
    24 July 2018, https://thehill.com/homenews/senate/398681-booker-those
    -who-dont-oppose-kavanaugh-are-complicit-in-the-evil.
2   Charles Lane, "We're Staying Silent Out of Fear," *Washington Post*, 15
    October 2018, https://www.washingtonpost.com/opinions/we-need-the
    -exhausted-majority-to-speak-up/2018/10/15/160440fa-d090-11e8-83d6
    -291fcead2ab1_story.html.
3   James Madison, *Federalist 51*; Madison, *Speech to the Virginia Ratifying
    Convention on the Control of the Military*, 16 June 1788, reprinted in *Madison:
    Writings* (New York: Library of America, 1999), pp. 294–6, 389.
4   *Trop v. Dulles*, 356 U.S. 86 (1958).
5   "The Constitution Turns 225 with Clarence Thomas and Akhil Amar,"
    Federalist Society, National Archives and Records Administration, and the
    Constitutional Accountability Center, 21 September 2012, https://fedsoc.
    org/commentary/videos/the-constitution-turns-225-with-clarence-thomas
    -event-audio-video.
6   A.L. Higginbotham Jr., "An Open Letter to Justice Clarence Thomas from a
    Federal Judicial Colleague," *University of Pennsylvania Law Review*, vol. 140,
    no. 3 (1992): p. 1005.
7   Edmund Burke, "Speech on Conciliation with the Colonies," 22 March
    1775, reprinted in *Select Works of Edmund Burke*, ed. E.J. Payne, vol. 1
    (Indianapolis: Liberty Fund, 1999), 237, 239.
8   V.S. Naipaul, "Our Universal Civilization," *City Journal* (Summer 1991),
    https://www.city-journal.org/html/our-universal-civilization-12753.html.
9   Clarence Thomas, *My Grandfather's Son: A Memoir* (New York:
    HarperCollins, 2007), p. 282.

CHAPTER TWO: THE MAKING OF A JUSTICE

1   Clarence Thomas, Joseph Story Distinguished Lecture, Heritage
    Foundation, 26 October 2016, https://www.heritage.org/courts/event/the
    -joseph-story-distinguished-lecture-justice-clarence-thomas.

2   Richard Brookhiser, *Founders' Son: A Life of Abraham Lincoln* (New York:
    Basic Books, 2014).

3   Thomas, *My Grandfather's Son*, pp. 6, 8.

4   Thomas, *My Grandfather's Son*, pp. 10, 2.

5   Thomas, *My Grandfather's Son*, pp. 12–13, 19, 26–7, 60, 169.

6   "The Constitution Turns 225 with Clarence Thomas and Akhil Amar";
    Thomas, *My Grandfather's Son*, p. 15.

7   "The Constitution Turns 225 with Clarence Thomas and Akhil Amar."

8   Juan Williams, "Black Conservatives, Center Stage," *Washington
    Post*, 16 December 1980, https://www.washingtonpost.com/archive/
    politics/1980/12/16/black-conservatives-center-stage/c5b44552-ad84-4a40
    -9b3c-3e88fdfa3589.

9   Kevin Merida and Michael A. Fletcher, *Supreme Discomfort: The Divided
    Soul of Clarence Thomas* (New York: Broadway Books, 2007), pp. 38–40.

10 Thomas, Story Lecture.

11 Clarence Thomas, The Gregory S. Coleman Memorial Lecture, Federalist
    Society Texas Conference, 7 September 2018, https://fedsoc.org/
    conferences/2018-texas-chapters-conference?#agenda-item-gregory-s
    -coleman-memorial-lecture-justice-clarence-thomas.

12 Thomas, *My Grandfather's Son*, p. 30.

13 Thomas, *My Grandfather's Son*, pp. 33, 37.

14 Juan Williams, "A Question of Fairness," *The Atlantic*, February 1987, https://
    www.theatlantic.com/magazine/archive/1987/02/a-question-of-fairness
    /306370.

15 Thomas, *My Grandfather's Son*, pp. 35–6, 34.

16 Clarence Thomas, Speech to National Bar Association, Memphis, TN, July
    28, 1998, http://teachingamericanhistory.org/library/document/speech-to
    -the-national-bar-association.

17 Thomas, *My Grandfather's Son*, pp. 48, 50–1.

18 Clarence Thomas, James M. McClure Memorial Lecture in Law, October 19,
    1995, reprinted in *Mississippi Law Journal*, vol. 65 (Spring 1996): pp. 463–75.

19 Thomas, *My Grandfather's Son*, pp. 54, 56.

20 Thomas, *My Grandfather's Son*, p. 60; "An Interview with Justice Clarence
    Thomas," National Lawyers Convention, 14 November 2013, https://fedsoc.
    org/commentary/videos/an-interview-with-justice-clarence-thomas-event
    -audio-video; Merida and Fletcher, *Supreme Discomfort*, p. 106.

21 Williams, "A Question of Fairness"; Williams, "Black Conservatives, Center
    Stage."

22 Thomas, *My Grandfather's Son*, pp. 78–80, 231–2.

23   Clarence Thomas, "Judgment," speech at University of Kansas Law School,
     8 April 1996, https://www.c-span.org/video/?72268-1/judgment-process;
     Williams, "A Question of Fairness."

24   Thomas, *My Grandfather's Son*, pp. 99–100.

25   Williams, "A Question of Fairness."

26   Thomas, *My Grandfather's Son*, pp. 94–5.

27   Thomas, *My Grandfather's Son*, pp. 106–7.

28   Merida and Fletcher, *Supreme Discomfort*, p. 120.

29   Thomas, *My Grandfather's Son*, pp. 118, 169.

30   Thomas, *My Grandfather's Son*, p. 130.

31   Thomas, *My Grandfather's Son*, p. 138.

32   Thomas, *My Grandfather's Son*, pp. 142–3, 163–4.

33   Williams, "A Question of Fairness."

34   Williams, "A Question of Fairness."

35   Williams, "A Question of Fairness."

36   Williams, "A Question of Fairness."

37   Thomas, *My Grandfather's Son*, p. 188; Kenneth Masugi, personal
     communication with author, summer 2017.

38   Abraham Lincoln, "Eulogy on Henry Clay," 6 July 1852; "Speech at
     Springfield, Illinois," 17 July 1858; both reprinted in *Lincoln: Speeches and
     Writings, 1832–1858* (New York: Library of America, 1989), pp. 269, 477–8.

39   C. Boyden Gray, "25 Years of Justice Clarence Thomas," 28 June 2016, in
     Federalist Society, podcast, https://fedsoc.org/commentary/podcasts/25
     -years-of-justice-clarence-thomas-podcast; Thomas, *My Grandfather's Son*,
     pp. 199–201.

40   Merida and Fletcher, *Supreme Discomfort*, p. 178.

41   John C. Danforth, *Resurrection: The Confirmation of Clarence Thomas* (New
     York: Viking Penguin, 1994), pp. 196, 11–12, 2, 8, 133.

42   Danforth, *Resurrection*, pp. 10, 11.

43   Ron Chernow, *Washington: A Life* (New York: Penguin, 2010), pp. 590–3.

44   Thomas, *My Grandfather's Son*, p. 221.

45   Merida and Fletcher, *Supreme Discomfort*, p. 179; Danforth, *Resurrection*,
     p. 36; Anna Miller, ed., *The Complete Transcripts of the Clarence Thomas–
     Anita Hill Hearings* (Chicago: Academy Chicago Publishers, 1994), pp. 96–7,
     172, 294.

46   Danforth, *Resurrection*, pp. 120–1.

47   Miller, *Clarence Thomas–Anita Hill Hearings*, p. 209.

48   Miller, *Clarence Thomas–Anita Hill Hearings*, p. 92.

49   Thomas, *My Grandfather's Son*, pp. 273–4; Miller, *Clarence Thomas–Anita
     Hill Hearings*, pp. 158–61.

50   Thomas, *My Grandfather's Son*, pp. 245, 261–5; Danforth, *Resurrection*,
     pp. 74–5.

51   Danforth, *Resurrection*, pp. 154, 170–1; Miller, *Clarence Thomas–Anita Hill
     Hearings*, pp. 288, 56.

52 Merida and Fletcher, *Supreme Discomfort*, p. 207.
53 Merida and Fletcher, *Supreme Discomfort*, p. 208.
54 Merida and Fletcher, *Supreme Discomfort*, p. 201.

CHAPTER THREE: WHO KILLED THE CONSTITUTION?

1   Brookhiser, *Founders' Son*, p. 291.
2   Allen C. Guelzo, *Reconstruction: A Concise History* (New York: Oxford, 2018), pp. 15–16, 19–26.
3   Guelzo, *Reconstruction*, pp. 35–7.
4   Guelzo, *Reconstruction*, pp. 40, 49–53, 56–7.
5   Ron Chernow, *Grant* (New York: Penguin, 2017), pp. 228–31; Guelzo, *Reconstruction*, p. 70.
6   Guelzo, *Reconstruction*, pp. 67–8, 72; Gene Dattel, *Reckoning with Race: America's Failure* (New York: Encounter, 2017), pp. 15–16, 27–33, 47, 51–2, 29–30.
7   Nicholas Lemann, *Redemption: The Last Battle of the Civil War* (New York: Farrar, Straus and Giroux, 2006), pp. 63, 49, 93–4.
8   Guelzo, *Reconstruction*, pp. 71, 74–5; W.E.B. Du Bois, *Black Reconstruction in America, 1860–1880* (New York: Free Press, 1998), p. 190.
9   Charles Dickens, *American Notes* (1842), ch. 9.
10 Guelzo, *Reconstruction*, p. 76.
11 Guelzo, *Reconstruction*, pp. 42, 73; Dattel, *Reckoning with Race*, p. 44.
12 Guelzo, *Reconstruction*, pp. 45, 12.
13 Guelzo, *Reconstruction*, p. 130.
14 Guelzo, *Reconstruction*, p. 95.
15 Lemann, *Redemption*, pp. 6–7, 12, 14–19.
16 Lemann, *Redemption*, pp. 20–1.
17 *The Slaughter-House Cases*, 83 U.S. 36 (1873); Richard Epstein, *The Classical Liberal Constitution: The Uncertain Quest for Limited Government* (Cambridge, MA: Harvard University Press, 2014), pp. 308, 528–31.
18 Thomas, Story Lecture.
19 *United States v. Cruikshank et al.*, 92 U.S. 542 (1876).
20 Thomas Jefferson, *Writings* (New York: Library of America, 1984), p. 245; James Madison to Spencer Roane, 2 September 1819, https://founders.archives.gov/documents/Madison/04-01-02-0455.
21 Woodrow Wilson, *The New Freedom*, in *American Progressivism: A Reader*, ed. Ronald J. Pestritto and William J. Atto (Lanham, MD: Lexington Books, 2008), pp. 50–1.
22 Abraham Lincoln, *First Inaugural Address*, 4 March 1861, in Lincoln, *Speeches and Writings 1859–1865* (New York: Library of America, 1989), p. 221.
23 Wilson, *The New Freedom*, p. 53.
24 Ronald Pestritto, "The Birth of the Administrative State: Where It Came From and What It Means for Limited Government," Heritage Foundation

Report, 20 November 2007, https://www.heritage.org/political-process/
report/the-birth-the-administrative-state-where-it-came-and-what-it
-means-limited.

25 Pestritto, "The Birth of the Administrative State"; Woodrow Wilson,
    Constitutional Government in the United States (New York: Columbia
    University Press, 1911), p. 16.

26 Philip Hamburger, *Is Administrative Law Unlawful?* (Chicago: University of
    Chicago Press, 2014), pp. 448, 451–3, 455, 457–61, 464–74.

27 *Railroad Retirement Board v. Alton R.R.*, 295 U.S. 330 (1935).

28 *A.L.A. Schechter Poultry Corp. v. U.S.*, 295 U.S. 495 (1935).

29 *Carter v. Carter Coal Co.*, 298 U.S. 238 (1936).

30 *NLRB v. Jones & Laughlin Steel Corp.*, 301 U.S. 1 (1937); Epstein, *Classical
    Liberal Constitution*, p. 170.

31 *United States v. Darby*, 312 U.S. 100 (1941).

32 *Wickard v. Filburn*, 317 U.S. 111 (1942).

33 George B. Shepherd, "Fierce Compromise: The Administrative Procedure
    Act Emerges from New Deal Politics," 90 *Northwestern Law Review* 1557,
    1558 (1996).

34 John Marini, "Abandoning the Constitution," *Claremont Review of Books*, vol.
    7, no. 2 (Spring 2012), http://www.claremont.org/crb/article/abandoning
    -the-constitution.

35 Hamburger, *Is Administrative Law Unlawful?*, pp. 381–2, 124–7.

36 Shepherd, "Fierce Compromise"; Hamburger, *Is Administrative Law
    Unlawful?*, pp. 227, 234–7.

37 Shepherd, "Fierce Compromise."

38 Todd Gaziano and Tommy Berry, "Career Civil Servants Illegitimately Rule
    America," *Wall Street Journal*, 28 February 2018.

39 *Humphrey's Executor v. United States*, 295 U.S. 602 (1935).

40 Shepherd, "Fierce Compromise."

41 Chernow, *Washington*, p. 590; FDR to Luther C. Steward, 16 August 1937,
    https://www.presidency.ucsb.edu/documents/letter-the-resolution
    -federation-federal-employees-against-strikes-federal-service.

42 *Confessions of Congressman X* (Minneapolis: Mill City Press, 2016);
    Pew Research Center, "Public Trust in Government 1958–2017," 14
    December 2017, http://www.people-press.org/2017/12/14/public-trust-in-
    government-1958-2017.

43 Edmund Morris, *The Rise of Theodore Roosevelt* (New York: Random House,
    1979), p. 124.

44 *Brown v. Board of Education of Topeka*, 347 U.S. 483 (1954).

45 *Brown v. Board of Education of Topeka (2)*, 349 U.S. 294 (1955).

46 *Green v. County School Board of New Kent County*, 391 U.S. 430 (1968);
    Swann v. Charlotte-Mecklenburg Board of Education, 402 U.S. 1 (1971).

47 *Keyes v. School District No. 1, Denver, Colorado*, 413 U.S. 189 (1973).

48 Richard E. Morgan, *Disabling America: The "Rights Industry" in Our Time*

(New York: Basic Books, 1984), pp. 50–7, 145–51; Myron Magnet, *The Founders at Home: The Building of America, 1735–1817* (New York: Norton, 2014), pp. 266–7, 276–82.

49 *Roe v. Wade*, 410 U.S. 113 (1973).

50 *Griswold v. Connecticut*, 381 U.S. 479 (1965).

51 Megan McArdle, "Let Roe Go," *Washington Post*, 3 July 2018.

CHAPTER FOUR: ORIGINALISM IN ACTION

1 Thomas, "Judgment," speech at University of Kansas Law School.

2 Thomas, Story Lecture; Thomas, Coleman Lecture.

3 *United States v. Lopez*, 514 U.S. 549 (1995).

4 *Wickard v. Filburn*, 317 U.S. 111 (1942).

5 *Gonzalez v. Raich*, 545 U.S. 1 (2005); *National Federation of Independent Business v. Sebelius*, 567 U.S. 519 (2012).

6 Dahlia Lithwick and Mark Joseph Stern, "The Clarence Thomas Takeover," *Slate*, 2 August 2017, https://slate.com/news-and-politics/2017/08/clarence -thomas-legal-vision-is-becoming-a-trump-era-reality.html; Gregory G. Katsas, "25 Years of Justice Clarence Thomas," 28 June 2016, in *Federalist Society*, podcast, https://fedsoc.org/commentary/podcasts/25-years-of- justice-clarence-thomas-podcast.

7 *Department of Transportation v. Association of American Railroads*, 575 U.S. ___ (2015).

8 Dianne Feinstein, "Feinstein Speaks at Supreme Court Nomination Hearing," press release, 20 March 2017, https://www.feinstein.senate.gov/ public/index.cfm/press-releases?ID=745D797F-76F1-4EB0-8ACD- 388BDA95A4D8.

9 Morgan, *Disabling America*, pp. 146–7, 140.

10 *Bowles v. Seminole Rock & Sand*, 325 U.S. 410 (1945); *Perez v. Mortgage Bankers Association*, 575 U.S. ___ (2015).

11 Thomas, Story Lecture.

12 *Michigan v. EPA*, 576 U.S. ___ (2015); *Chevron v. Natural Resources Defense Council*, 467 U.S. 837 (1984); *Marbury v. Madison*, 5 U.S. 137 (1803).

13 Lithwick and Stern, "The Clarence Thomas Takeover"; Linda Greenhouse, "Is Clarence Thomas the Supreme Court's Future?," *New York Times*, 2 August 2018.

14 *McDonald v. Chicago*, 561 U.S. 742 (2010).

15 Juan Williams, "America's Most Influential Thinker on Race," *Wall Street Journal*, 20 February 2015, https://www.wsj.com/articles/juan-williams- americas-most-influential-thinker-on-race-1424476527.

16 *Adarand Constructors, Inc. v. Peña*, 515 U.S. 200 (1995).

17 *Missouri v. Jenkins*, 515 U.S. 70 (1995).

18 Clarence Thomas, "An Afro-American Perspective: Toward a 'Plain Reading' of the Constitution—The Declaration of Independence in Constitutional Interpretation," *Howard Law Journal*, vol. 30 (1987): pp. 698–700.

19   Thomas Jefferson to Philip Mazzei, November 1785, https://founders. archives.gov/documents/Jefferson/01-09-02-0056.

20   *Grutter v. Bollinger*, 539 U.S. 306 (2003).

21   Clarence Thomas, "Punishment and Personhood," *City Journal* (Autumn 1994), https://www.city-journal.org/html/punishment-and -personhood-12528.html.

22   *Papachristou v. City of Jacksonville*, 405 U.S. 156 (1972).

23   *City of Chicago v. Morales*, 527 U.S. 41 (1999).

24   *In re Gault*, 387 U.S. 1 (1967); Morgan, *Disabling America*, pp. 64–6.

25   *Tinker v. Des Moines Independent Community School District*, 393 U.S. 503 (1969).

26   *Morse v. Frederick*, 551 U.S. 393 (2007).

27   *Goss v. Lopez*, 419 U.S. 565 (1975); *Wood v. Strickland*, 420 U.S. 308 (1975); Morgan, *Disabling America*, pp. 67–8.

28   *Zelman v. Simmons-Harris*, 536 U.S. 639 (2002).

29   *Carpenter v. United States*, 585 U.S. _____ (2018).

30   *Olmstead v. United States*, 277 U.S. 438 (1928).

31   *Katz v. United States*, 389 U.S. 347 (1867).

32   *Cincinnati v. Discovery Network*, 507 U.S. 410 (1993); Ralph A. Rossum, *Understanding Clarence Thomas: The Jurisprudence of Constitutional Restoration* (Lawrence: University Press of Kansas, 2014), p. 101.

33   *Central Hudson Gas & Electric Corp. v. Public Service Commission*, 447 U.S. 557 (1980); *Rubin v. Coors Brewing Co.*, 514 U.S. 476 (1995).

34   *44 Liquormart, Inc. v. Rhode Island*, 517 U.S. 484 (1996); *Virginia State Pharmacy Board v. Virginia Citizens Consumer Council*, 425 U.S. 748 (1976).

35   Bradley A. Smith, "Why Campaign Finance Reform Never Works," *Wall Street Journal*, 19 March 1997.

36   Adam Liptak, "Justice Defends Ruling on Finance," *New York Times*, 3 February 2010.

37   Bradley A. Smith, "The Myth of Campaign Finance Reform," *National Affairs* (Summer 2018).

38   *Nixon v. Shrink Missouri Government PAC*, 528 U.S. 377 (2000).

39   *McConnell v. Federal Election Commission*, 540 U.S. 93 (2003); *Austin v. Michigan Chamber of Commerce*, 494 U.S. 652 (1990).

40   Smith, "The Myth of Campaign Finance Reform."

41   Magnet, *Founders at Home*, ch. 1.

42   *McIntyre v. Ohio Elections Commission*, 514 U.S. 334 (1995); Bernard Bailyn, *The Ideological Origins of the American Revolution*, enlarged ed. (Cambridge, MA: Harvard University Press, 1967).

43   *Citizens United v. Federal Election Commission*, 558 U.S. 310 (2010).

44   John Jay to Peter Jay Munroe in William Jay, *The Life of John Jay*, vol. 2 (1833; rpt. Bridgewater, VA: American Foundation Publications, 2000), 348–9.

45   *Fallbrook Irrigation District v. Bradley*, 164 U.S. 112 (1896); Kay Russell, "The Fallbrook Irrigation District Case," *San Diego Historical Society Quarterly*, vol.

21, no. 2 (Spring 1975), http://www.sandiegohistory.org/journal/1975/april/
fallbrook.

46 *Berman v. Parker*, 348 U.S. 26 (1954).

47 *Hawaii Housing Authority v. Midkiff*, 467 U.S. 229 (1984).

48 *Kelo v. City of New London*, 545 U.S. 469 (2005).

49 *Webster v. Reproductive Health Services*, 492 U.S. 490 (1989); *Planned
    Parenthood v. Casey*, 505 U.S. 833 (1992).

50 *Stenberg v. Carhart*, 530 U.S. 914 (2000).

51 *Gonzales v. Carhart*, 550 U.S. 124 (2007).

52 Carey Goldberg, "Shots Assist in Aborting Fetuses," *Boston Globe*, 10
    August 2007, http://archive.boston.com/yourlife/health/women/
    articles/2007/08/10/shots_assist_in_aborting_fetuses/?page=1.

CHAPTER FIVE: "A FREE MAN"

1   Higginbotham, "An Open Letter to Justice Clarence Thomas," p. 1005.

2   Juan Williams, "EEOC Chairman Blasts Black Leaders," *Washington
    Post*, 25 October 1984, https://www.washingtonpost.com/archive/
    politics/1984/10/25/eeoc-chairman-blasts-black-leaders/1f7fe039-e807-
    48ca-a92c-fd7bfcba3345; Higginbotham, "An Open Letter to Justice
    Clarence Thomas."

3   Thomas, Speech to National Bar Association; https://www.c-span.org/
    video/?109490-1/supreme-court-justice-speech.

4   Magnet, *Founders at Home*, pp. 323–7, 17–18, 30–8.

5   Thomas, McClure Lecture.

6   Clarence Thomas, Churchill Statesmanship Prize Speech, Claremont
    Institute, 20 November 1993, https://www.c-span.org/video/?52523-1/
    supreme-court-justice-perspective.

7   Thomas, McClure Lecture.

8   Thomas, Coleman Lecture.

9   Thomas, McClure Lecture.

10 Thomas, Churchill Statesmanship Prize Speech.

11 Magnet, *Founders at Home*, p. 183.

12 "The Constitution Turns 225 with Clarence Thomas and Akhil Amar."

13 Thomas, McClure Lecture.

14 Thomas, "Punishment and Personhood."

15 Thomas, "Punishment and Personhood."

16 Thomas, McClure Lecture; *Goldberg v. Kelly*, 397 U.S. 254 (1970).

17 Thomas, McClure Lecture.

18 U.S. Census Bureau, Current Population Survey, Annual Social and
    Economic Supplement, Table POV-26 (2016), https://www.census.gov/
    data/tables/time-series/demo/income-poverty/cps-pov/pov-26.2016.html.

19 Thomas, "Punishment and Personhood."

20 Alexis de Tocqueville, *Democracy in America*, trans. Arthur Goldhammer (New York: Library of America, 2004), pp. 60, 757–8, 293.

21 Tocqueville, *Democracy in America*, pp. 294, 284, 493.

22 Tocqueville, *Democracy in America*, pp. 46, 80, 65, 215–16.

23 Tocqueville, *Democracy in America*, p. 301.

24 Alexis de Tocqueville, *The Old Regime and the French Revolution*, trans. Stuart Gilbert (Garden City, NY: Doubleday Anchor, 1955), pp. 57, 40–1, 190, 51; Tocqueville, *Democracy in America*, p. 809.

25 Tocqueville, *The Old Regime and the French Revolution*, pp. 66, 62, 58.

26 Tocqueville, *Democracy in America*, pp. 141, 106–7, 105.

27 Tocqueville, *Democracy in America*, p. 790.

28 Tocqueville, *Democracy in America*, pp. 809, 597.

29 Tocqueville, *Democracy in America*, p. 818.

30 Tocqueville, *Democracy in America*, pp. 818–19.

31 Tocqueville, *Democracy in America*, p. 804; Thomas, McClure Lecture.

32 Tocqueville, *Democracy in America*, pp. 820, 802.

33 Quoted in Greg Lukianoff and Jonathan Haidt, "The Coddling of the American Mind," *The Atlantic* (September 2015), https://www.theatlantic.com/magazine/archive/2015/09/the-coddling-of-the-american-mind/399356.

34 Thomas, Churchill Statesmanship Prize Speech.

35 Barack Obama, *Dreams from My Father: A Story of Race and Inheritance* (1995; New York: Three Rivers Press, 2004), p. 16.

36 Barack Obama, *The Audacity of Hope: Thoughts on Reclaiming the American Dream* (New York: Three Rivers Press, 2006), p. 346.

37 Obama, *Dreams from My Father*, pp. 76, 79.

38 Obama, *Dreams from My Father*, pp. 85, 87, 101, 4.

39 Obama, *Dreams from My Father*, pp. 177–8, 229, 253, 260–1; Obama, *The Audacity of Hope*, pp. 255, 252–3.

40 Obama, *Dreams from My Father*, pp. 286, 194.

41 Barack Obama, "Remarks by the President on Trayvon Martin," White House, 19 July 2013, https://obamawhitehouse.archives.gov/the-press-office/2013/07/19/remarks-president-trayvon-martin.

42 Barack Obama, Speech in Warsaw, 7 July 2016, http://time.com/4397600/obama-alton-sterling-philando-castile-speech-transcript.

43 Ta-Nehisi Coates, "'Better Is Good': Obama on Reparations, Civil Rights, and the Art of the Possible," *The Atlantic*, 21 December 2016, https://www.theatlantic.com/politics/archive/2016/12/ta-nehisi-coates-obama-transcript-ii/511133.

44 Barack Obama, "Remarks by the President at a Campaign Event in Roanoke, Virginia," White House, 13 July 2012, https://obamawhitehouse.archives.gov/the-press-office/2012/07/13/remarks-president-campaign-event-roanoke-virginia; Obama, *The Audacity of Hope*, pp. 155, 90.

45 Williams, "A Question of Fairness."

46 "The Constitution Turns 225 with Clarence Thomas and Akhil Amar."

47 Merida and Fletcher, *Supreme Discomfort*, p. 21.

48 "The Constitution Turns 225 with Clarence Thomas and Akhil Amar"; "An Interview with Justice Clarence Thomas."

Index